TRAVEL

A Guide to Healthy Travelling Overseas

Dr Graham Fry and Dr Vincent Kenny

Newleaf

Newleaf
an imprint of
Gill & Macmillan Ltd
Hume Avenue
Park West
Dublin 12
with associated companies throughout the world
www.gillmacmillan.ie

© 2000 Dr Graham Fry and Dr Vincent Kenny
0 7171 2988 8
Index compiled by Helen Litton
Print origination by Carole Lynch
Printed by Caledonian International Book Manufacturing Ltd, Glasgow

A catalogue record is available for this book
from the British Library.

5 4 3 2 1

Contents

Introduction   v

SECTION 1   BEFORE YOU TRAVEL   1
Getting Ready   3
Useful Charts
    Electricity and Voltages of the World   6
    Temperatures   9
    Rainfall   11
    Time Zones   13
Countries Infected with
    Malaria   14
    Yellow Fever   16
    Cholera   18
First-aid List   20
Vaccines   22
Hints for Healthy Travelling
    while pregnant   31
    with children   33
    with diabetes   34
    with asthma   36
    with heart disease   37
The Traveller's Checklist   38

SECTION 2   WHILE ABROAD   43
Jetlag and How to Cope   45
Food-borne Disease   48
Water-borne Disease   55
Insect-borne Disease   60
The Risk of Malaria   67
Swimming on Holiday   74

Sun Exposure   79
The Risk of Rabies   84
Snakes, Spiders and Scorpions   90
Problems at Altitude   93
The Trekking Holiday   98
Sexually Transmitted Disease   102
How to Treat
    diarrhoea   105
    sunburn   106
    fever   106
    diarrhoea, nausea and vomiting   107
Medical Attention Overseas   109

SECTION 3 AFTER YOU RETURN   111
What to Look Out For   113
The Medical Check   118
Your Next Trip   120

APPENDICES   121
Northern Africa   123
Sub-Saharan Africa   124
Southern Africa   126
North America   127
Central America   128
Caribbean Region   129
Tropical South America   130
Temperate South America   132
East Asia   133
Eastern South Asia   134
Middle/South Asia   135
Western South Asia   136
Northern Europe   137
Southern Europe   138
Australasia   139
Melanesia and Micronesia-Polynesia   140
Index   141

INTRODUCTION

There is little doubt that people today are travelling in a way that previous generations would have regarded with utter amazement. We walk into a rather large metal cylinder, a plane, and a few hours later we are deposited many miles from home. We have the opportunity to see, experience and explore regions of our world that in the past most people could only have dreamed about. This newfound ability to travel the world brings with it many pleasures but also some dangers, which may not always be self-evident. When we return from our travels we may carry with us not only memories of visits to distant places but, perhaps, some unwanted visitors in the form of intestinal or blood parasites. These may not cause symptoms until weeks or even months after we get back. Not a pleasant thought!

New countries, even regions within countries, may present risks to the traveller's health, which need to be considered and dealt with in whatever is the most appropriate way. The range of illness to which we may subject ourselves varies from mild flu to a severe bout of bacillary dysentery. Of course even more life-threatening diseases can affect the traveller. The major diseases of the world have names most people will never have heard of, such as trypanosomiasis, leishmaniasis, schistosomiasis and malaria. These diseases, and many more, kill millions of people each year and are found throughout the tropics. Don't despair! We can help you stay free of these and many other diseases as you travel the world.

Even milder diseases can be significant, especially if you have saved for months to take a holiday and then suddenly you are sick and stuck in the smallest room of the hotel for an unacceptable period of time. Was all the saving worth it? Of course it was, but first you must learn some basic common-sense rules and realise that staying healthy while abroad means following these rules not just some of the time but all the time. Where and what to eat and drink, when to use sunblocking lotions, and how to avoid bites and stings, snakes, scorpions, insects or dogs — there are some simple rules and they are all worth considering before you get sick rather than afterwards!

The following chapters aim to cover the major pitfalls into which travellers tend to fall while overseas. This short book cannot be all-inclusive but it does seek to cover the main causes of illnesses for the short-term traveller. Whether you propose a sun-soaking holiday in southern Europe, a trekking safari through Africa or a business trip to Asia, illness can upset even the best-laid plans. Don't think of yourself as immune, disaster can strike at any time so take care with your most precious gift, your health.

So how should we write a book about the joys and excitement of foreign travel and yet warn of the real risks to health? Should we specifically describe the world, region by region, in terms of disease profile? No, for this would not only alarm but give a misleading impression of the beauty and happiness which most people experience on their foreign holiday. Also, the major cities of the world, whether they are in Asia, Africa, Europe or the Americas, are all similar in the respective ways, despite their cultural and climatic differences. Follow us, then, on a journey around the world and let us show you some of the common health pitfalls, how to avoid them and how to experience the real joy of those who travel in health.

Before You Travel

GETTING READY

They say that a change is as good as a rest, but there can be nothing quite like getting away from it all. Sitting down in the aeroplane and heading off into the blue yonder — that's the life! So now that you have made a general decision that a holiday is what is needed, you need to get yourself organised. Plan the build-up for your trip so that everything will run smoothly and then there should be no last-minute hitches, or at least as few as possible.

Choosing the destination

Knowing what you want from the holiday is all-important. Some travellers delight in an energetic holiday while others just want to flop down beside the sea and do nothing. Make a general decision and then discuss the possibilities with the travel agent. Don't forget, in many of the better travel agencies, the staff will have visited the destinations and will be able to give you an up-to-date and accurate rundown on the hotels and the amenities close by.

Tell the travel agent of any special requirements you may have and ask their advice. Don't forget to listen to what they say. If you have arthritis don't end up with a room on the fifth floor in a liftless hotel. If you love swimming don't find yourself miles from the beach in a hotel without a swimming pool.

Make a list of what you want available at your destination. Mark the essential items and others that would be nice but you could live without.

If you are planning an apartment holiday, ask how far the nearest shops are from site.

Check if your hotel is miles from the nearest town, and what the cost would be to hire a taxi.

If you have arthritis or a heart condition check if the region is very hilly and how many steps there are up to the hotel; ask if you could book a room on a lower floor. If you are in a wheelchair ask if there are easy access points and other facilities.

Spending a few minutes asking these pertinent questions will help you to enjoy your holiday so much more. Go on, make that list of requirements now!

Visa and vaccine requirements

Again your travel agent will be able to help you here. Often a holiday visa is available at the point of entry. Phone or write to the embassy or consulate and make certain that the duration of your journey does not push you out of the holiday visa category. Bring a few passport-size photographs with you just in case these do become necessary to obtain a visa upon entry.

Details regarding vaccination advice are available from your local travel vaccination clinic. Travellers often ask what vaccines are essential for their holiday. Frequently there will be no essential vaccines but some would be recommended for personal protection. The vaccine advice will be linked with other vital information regarding food- and water-borne disease so this makes the visit to the centre well worth while. Know your itinerary and make a list of the questions you would like to have answered. If you are particularly prone to illness, or severe allergic reactions, ask for the names of English-speaking doctors in the area you plan to visit. All of these will help you stay well for your trip, but mind you if you have read *Travel in Health* you should at least be well prepared!

Where necessary, vaccinations would usually be given on one or two occasions before your trip. Try to plan the first visit at least four weeks before you leave if you are off on a short holiday. If you are going on a longer trip, try to plan at least eight to twelve weeks ahead.

First-aid kits

Most travellers should throw together some odds and ends even for the shortest trips overseas. A few paracetamol can be life-saving for toothache, sunburn or the twisted ankle. An outline for a first-aid kit is included on pp. 20–21.

Medical check

For many travellers it will be unnecessary to have a full medical check before their trip. However, for others a trip to their doctor a month or so before they leave (perhaps even before they finally book and pay for their holiday) may be very worth while.

The main group of otherwise healthy travellers who will benefit from a medical check are those planning to go up very high and those planning to go down very low! The risk of altitude sickness is outlined on pp. 93–7. Scuba-diving is also becoming popular and it is essential that divers know that their ears are perfect before this sport is undertaken. Any traveller with a history of 'ear problems' or who is subject to 'panic attacks' should really think twice before going down to any significant depth. In fact many of the more reputable diving companies will insist on a clear medical certificate before allowing you take part.

Bits and pieces

On the following pages there are some lists which may be of help in planning your luggage for the journey.

Will your razor work?

How hot does it become?

When does it rain?

What time zone will you be in?

Does malaria transmission occur?

Do you need vaccination against yellow fever?

What about cholera?

Check the lists for your destination.

ELECTRICITY AND VOLTAGES OF THE WORLD

Check the electrical and voltage systems that are available in your destination to see if your appliances will work.

Country	Voltage	Country	Voltage	Country	Voltage
Afghanistan	220v	Burkina Faso	220v	Egypt	220v
Albania	220v	Burma (Myanmar)	220v	El Salvador	110v
Algeria	220v	Burundi	220v	Ethiopia	220v
Angola	220v	Cambodia	220v	Falkland Is.	240v
Argentina	220v	Cameroon	220v	Fiji	240v
Australia	240v	Canada	110/120v	Finland	220v
Austria	220v	Canary Is.	220v	France	220v
Azores	220v	Cayman Is.	110v	French Guiana	120v
Bahamas	110/120v	Cent. African Rep.	220v	Fr. Polynesia	110v
Bahrain	240v	Chad	220v	Gabon	220v
Bali	220v	China	220v	Gambia	200v
Bangladesh	220v	Colombia	110v	Germany	220v
Barbados	110/120v	Congo	220v	Ghana	220v
Belgium	220v	Cook Is.	230v	Gibraltar	240v
Belize	220v	Corfu	220v	Greece	220v
Benin Rep.	220v	Corsica	220v	Grenada	220v
Bermuda	110/120v	Costa Rica	120v	Guatemala	110/120v
Bhutan	230v	Crete	220v	Guinea-Bissau	220v
Bolivia		Cuba	110/120v	Guinea Eq.	220v
La Paz	110v	Cyprus	240v	Guinea Rep.	220v
Elsewhere	220v	Czech Rep.	220v	Guyana	110v
Botswana	220v	Denmark	220v	Haiti	110v
Brazil	110/120v	Djibouti	220v	Hawaii	110/120v
Britain	240v	Dominican Rep.	110/120v	Honduras Rep.	110v
Brunei	220v	East Timor	220v	Hong Kong	220v
Bulgaria	220v	Ecuador	110/120v	Hungary	220v

Ibiza	220v	Mongolia	220v	Singapore	220v
Iceland	220v	Morocco	220v	Slovakia	220v
India	220v	Mozambique	220v	Solomon Is.	240v
Indonesia	220v	Myanmar (Burma)	220v	Somalia	220v
Iran	220v	Namibia	240v	South Africa	250v
Iraq	220v	Nepal	220v	Spain	220v
Ireland	240v	Netherlands	220v	Sri Lanka	230v
Israel	220v	Neth. Antilles	220v	Sudan	240v
Italy	220v	New Caledonia	220v	Surinam	110v
Ivory Coast	220v	New Zealand	230v	Swaziland	240v
Jamaica	110/120v	Nicaragua	110/120v	Sweden	220v
Japan	110/120v	Niger	220v	Switzerland	220v
Jordan	220v	Nigeria	240v	Syria	220v
Kenya	240v	Norway	220v	Taiwan	110/120v
Korea South	220v	Oman	220v	Tanzania	240v
Kuwait	240v	Pakistan	220v	Thailand	220v
Laos	220v	Panama	220v	Tobago	110/120v
Lebanon	220v	Papua New Guinea	240v	Togo	220v
Lesotho	220v	Paraguay	220v	Trinidad	110/120v
Liberia	240v	Peru	220v	Tunisia	220v
Libya	125v	Philippines	110/120v	Turkey	220v
Luxembourg	220v	Poland	220v	Uganda	240v
Madagascar	220v	Portugal	220v	United Arab Em.	220v
Madeira	220v	Puerto Rico	110v	Uruguay	220v
Majorca	220v	Qatar	240v	USA	110/120v
Malawi	240v	Reunion	110v	(Old) USSR	220v
Malaysia	220v	Romania	220v	Vanuatu	220v
Maldives	220v	Russia	220v	Venezuela	120v
Mali	220v	Rwanda	220v	Vietnam	220v
Malta	240v	St Lucia	220v	Yemen	220v
Martinique	220v	Samoa	220v	Yugoslavia	220v
Mauritania	220v	Sardinia	220v	Zaire	220v
Mauritius	240v	Saudi Arabia	220v	Zambia	240v
Mexico	110/120v	Senegal	110v	Zimbabwe	240v
Minorca	220v	Seychelles	240v		
Monaco	220v	Sierra Leone	240v		

It is only when you begin to pack that you realise how dependent we have all become on electrical gadgets. Razors, radios, torches, clocks, in fact almost every conceivable gadget you have is likely to be electrically dependent so check your appliance before you depart. Electricity comes in two basic forms, alternating current (AC) and direct current (DC). Many portable appliances incorporate both systems: that is, we can use batteries for them or the mains electric socket. Obviously the length of your overseas stay will dictate the number of batteries required. You will be amazed just how universal the standard 1.5-volt AA-type battery has become. This is certainly the best option if you have a choice.

The other possibility is to check if an electrical mains service is available. If it is, then the next question is what voltage is used in the area. Internationally there are two basic consumer voltage systems. The US standard (110–20) and the European system (220–40). In practical terms the voltage fluctuations within these two standards do not appear to affect the majority of modern electrical equipment. In fact many of our gadgets are now dual-standard and can be plugged in almost anywhere throughout the world. Nevertheless check it out before you go frying your laptop!

Despite the fact that all possible care has been taken to ensure that the figures above are correct, we cannot accept any liability for inaccuracies. If you require further information make sure you contact the appropriate embassy or consulate before you leave.

TEMPERATURES

The average summer and winter temperatures are given below in Fahrenheit for many of the main tourist destinations throughout the world. However, do remember that the 'El Niño' effect has resulted in changes and sometimes forecasting the weather can be fraught with difficulties.

Average January and July temperatures in Fahrenheit and Centigrade

	Jan.	July	Jan.	July
	Fahrenheit		Centigrade	
Alice Springs	83.5	53.0	28.6	11.6
Athens	48.0	81.0	8.8	27.2
Baghdad	49.5	93.0	9.7	33.8
Bahamas, Nassau	77.1	81.5	25.0	27.5
Beirut	56.5	80.0	13.6	26.6
Bombay	75.0	81.0	23.8	27.2
Buenos Aires	74.0	49.5	23.3	9.7
Cairo	56.0	83.0	13.3	28.3
Calcutta	67.5	84.0	19.7	28.8
Cape Town	69.0	54.0	20.5	12.2
Caracas	65.5	69.5	18.6	20.8
Chicago	25.0	73.5	−3.8	23.0
Christchurch, N.Z.	61.5	42.5	16.4	5.8
Cologne	36.0	65.5	2.2	18.6
Colombo	79.0	81.0	26.1	27.2
Darwin	83.5	77.0	28.6	25.0
Delhi	57.0	88.5	13.8	31.3
Funchal, Madeira	61.0	70.5	16.1	21.3
Geneva	34.0	67.5	1.1	19.7
Hamilton, Bermuda	63.0	79.0	17.2	26.1
Hong Kong	60.0	82.5	15.5	28.0

	Jan.	July	Jan.	July
	Fahrenheit		Centigrade	
Istanbul	40.5	73.0	4.7	22.7
Jerusalem	48.0	75.0	8.8	23.8
Johannesburg	68.0	51.0	20.0	10.5
Lagos	81.0	78.5	27.2	25.8
Lima	74.0	62.0	23.3	16.6
Livingstone	75.5	61.0	24.1	16.1
London	39.5	64.0	4.1	17.7
Los Angeles	55.5	70.5	13.0	21.4
Majorca	49.5	75.0	9.7	23.8
Mexico City	54.0	63.0	12.2	17.2
Miami	67.5	82.0	19.7	27.7
Mombasa	81.0	76.0	27.2	24.4
Moscow	15.0	65.5	−9.4	18.6
Nairobi	65.5	60.0	18.6	15.5
New York	30.5	74.0	−0.8	23.3
Oslo	25.0	64.5	−3.8	18.0
Paris	37.0	65.5	2.7	18.6
Rio de Janeiro	78.5	69.0	25.8	20.5
Rome	46.5	76.0	8.0	24.4
Singapore	79.5	81.5	26.4	27.5
Sydney	71.5	53.0	21.9	11.6
Tangier	53.5	72.0	11.9	22.2
Tokyo	38.0	76.5	3.3	24.7
Valparaiso, Chile	64.0	53.5	17.7	11.9
Winnipeg	−3.0	67.0	−18.3	19.4

RAINFALL

Knowing the extent of the rainfall in the region you wish to visit can be especially helpful as you try to pack your luggage. Nevertheless in many of the hotter areas throughout the world the rainfall tends to be both sporadic and torrential. If a sudden downpour does drown you, at least it is comforting to know that the higher ambient temperatures should dry you out soon.

Average January and July rainfall in inches and centimetres

	Jan.	July	Jan.	July
	Inches		Centimetres	
Alice Springs	1.7	0.3	4.3	0.8
Athens	2.2	0.2	5.6	0.5
Baghdad	0.9	<0.1	2.3	<0.2
Bahamas, Nassau	1.4	5.8	3.5	14.7
Beirut	7.5	<0.1	19.0	<0.2
Bombay	0.1	24.3	0.2	61.7
Buenos Aires	3.1	2.2	7.9	5.6
Cairo	0.2	0.0	0.5	0.0
Calcutta	0.4	12.8	1.0	32.5
Cape Town	0.6	3.5	1.5	8.9
Caracas	0.9	4.3	2.3	10.9
Chicago	2.0	3.3	5.0	8.4
Christchurch, N.Z.	2.2	2.7	5.6	6.8
Cologne	2.0	3.2	5.0	8.1
Colombo	3.5	5.3	8.9	13.5
Darwin	15.2	<0.1	38.6	<0.2
Delhi	0.9	7.1	2.3	18.0
Funchal, Madeira	2.5	<0.1	6.3	<0.2
Geneva	1.9	2.9	4.8	7.4
Hamilton, Bermuda	4.4	4.5	11.2	11.4

	Jan.	July	Jan.	July
	Inches		Centimetres	
Hong Kong	1.3	15.0	3.3	38.1
Istanbul	3.7	1.7	9.4	4.3
Jerusalem	5.2	0.0	13.2	0.0
Johannesburg	4.5	0.3	11.4	0.8
Lagos	1.1	11.0	2.8	27.9
Lima	<0.1	0.3	<0.2	0.8
Livingstone	5.7	0.0	14.5	0.0
London	2.0	2.0	5.0	5.0
Los Angeles	3.1	<0.1	7.9	<0.2
Majorca	1.4	0.2	3.5	0.5
Mexico City	0.5	6.7	1.3	17.0
Miami	2.8	6.1	7.1	15.5
Mombasa	1.0	3.5	2.5	8.9
Moscow	1.5	3.0	3.8	7.6
Nairobi	1.5	0.6	3.8	1.5
New York	3.7	4.2	9.4	10.7
Oslo	1.7	2.9	4.3	7.4
Paris	1.5	2.1	3.8	5.3
Rio de Janeiro	4.9	1.6	12.4	4.1
Rome	2.7	0.6	6.8	1.5
Singapore	9.9	6.7	25.1	17.0
Sydney	3.5	4.6	8.9	11.7
Tangier	4.5	<0.1	11.4	<0.2
Tokyo	1.9	5.6	4.8	14.2
Valparaiso, Chile	0.1	3.9	0.2	9.9
Winnipeg	0.9	3.1	2.3	7.9

TIME ZONES

It is essential to know how many time zones you will travel across in your journey. This is especially true if you have some stopovers during the flight. Adjusting your watch correctly is necessary if you don't want to miss your connections. However, remember that adjusting your watch to your new time zone does not mean that your body will automatically adjust as well; it won't! If you are flying for many hours you may well lose quite an amount of sleep as you cross the world's time zones so treat your body gently; you will need it later on! Generally you need one day to adapt for every one-hour time zone change. Some common destinations are shown and may be used as a guide, but remember to ask if there are any variations due to 'daylight saving time'. Where possible, fly towards the west as jetlag will be less. 'West is Best.'

Hours variation from Greenwich Mean Time (GMT)

Adelaide	+9.30	Harare	+2	Paris	+1
Anchorage	−9	Hong Kong	+8	Perth	+8
Athens	+2	Istanbul	+2	Quito	−5
Bangkok	+7	Jakarta	+7	Rio de Janeiro	−3
Beijing	+8	Johannesburg	+2	Riyadh	+3
Berlin	+1	Kinshasa	+1	Rome	+1
Bogotá	−5	Lagos	+1	Santiago	−5
Bombay	+5.30	Lima	−5	Seoul	+9
Buenos Aires	−3	Lisbon	GMT	Singapore	+7
Cairo	+2	Lusaka	+2	Stockholm	+1
Calcutta	+6.30	Madrid	+1	Sydney	+10
Cape Town	+2	Manila	+8	Tel Aviv	+3
Casablanca	GMT	Marrakesh	GMT	Tokyo	+9
Dakar	GMT	Mexico City	−6	Toronto	−5
Dublin	GMT	Moscow	+3	Tunis	+1
Durban	+2	Nairobi	+3	Wellington	+12
Gibraltar	+1	New York	−5		

MALARIA

One of the most significant risks for the international traveller is that they may be exposed to malaria during their time abroad. This is particularly true for those who may be travelling outside the major cities in the tropics. The chapter on the risk of malaria will give more information but the chart below indicates the countries which are currently infected with the disease and also those where there is a growing problem of resistance to the normal drugs which are used to protect us.

'R' denotes countries with resistant malaria. More countries are likely to report resistance. Request current information before your journey.

Afghanistan	R	China	R	Guyana	R
Algeria		Colombia	R	Haiti	
Angola	R	Comoros	R	Honduras Rep.	
Argentina		Congo	R	India	R
Azerbaijan		Costa Rica		Indonesia	R
Bangladesh	R	Dem. Rep. of Congo	R	Iran	R
Belize		Djibouti	R	Iraq	
Benin Rep.	R	Dominican Rep.		Ivory Coast	R
Bhutan	R	Ecuador	R	Kenya	R
Bolivia	R	Egypt		Laos	R
Botswana	R	El Salvador		Liberia	R
Brazil	R	Eritrea	R	Libya	
Burkina Faso	R	Ethiopia	R	Madagascar	R
Burma (Myanmar)	R	French Guiana	R	Malawi	R
Burundi	R	Gabon	R	Malaysia	R
Cambodia	R	Gambia	R	Mali	R
Cameroon	R	Ghana	R	Mauritania	R
Cape Verde Is.		Guatemala		Mauritius	
Cent. African Rep.	R	Guinea-Bissau	R	Mayotte	R
Chad	R	Guinea Eq.	R	Mexico	

Morocco		Philippines	R	Tajikistan	
Mozambique	R	Rwanda	R	Tanzania	R
Myanmar (Burma)	R	Sao Tomé	R	Thailand	R
Namibia	R	Saudi Arabia	R	Togo	R
Nepal	R	Senegal	R	Turkey	
Nicaragua		Sierra Leone	R	Uganda	R
Niger	R	Solomon Is.	R	United Arab Em.	
Nigeria	R	Somalia	R	Vanuatu	R
Oman	R	South Africa	R	Venezuela	R
Pakistan	R	Sri Lanka	R	Vietnam	R
Panama	R	Sudan	R	Yemen	R
Papua New Guinea	R	Surinam	R	Zambia	R
Paraguay		Swaziland	R	Zimbabwe	R
Peru	R	Syria			

(Source: World Health Organization International Travel and Health, 1999)

YELLOW FEVER

Saying that yellow fever is endemic to a country means that either transmission is known to occur there at present or the disease has been reported in the recent past. The incidence of yellow fever in travellers is extremely small but vaccination may be required for entry/exit purposes.

Yellow fever is a viral disease transmitted by the bite of an infected mosquito. The disease is mainly spread in Western Africa and parts of South America. Transmission has not been shown in Asia, despite the fact that the mosquito vectors do occur in this area and the climate is suitable. It is for this reason that some countries will insist on prior vaccination against yellow fever if the traveller has recently been through a region to which yellow fever is endemic. Check with your travel vaccination centre in plenty of time before you travel.

Africa

Angola: Provinces: Bengo and Luanda

Benin: Department: Atakora

Burkina Faso: Gaoua Region

Cameroon: Northern Province

Democratic Republic of Congo: North of 10° South

Gabon: Ogooué-Ivindo Province

Gambia: Upper River Division

Ghana: Upper West Region

Guinea: Siguiri Region

Liberia: Bassa County, Boma County, Bong County, Sinoe County

Nigeria: States: Anambra, Bauchi, Bendel, Benue, Cross River, Imo, Kaduna, Kwara, Lagos, Niger, Ogun, Ondo, Oyo and Plateau

Sierra Leone: Kenama District

Sudan: South of 12° North

South America

Bolivia: Departments: Beni, Cochabamba, La Paz and Santa Cruz

Brazil: Territories: Amapá; States: Amazonas, Maranhao, Pará

Colombia: Departments: Antioquia, Boyacá, César, Choco, Cundinamarca, Norte de Santander, Santander and Vichada; Intendencias: Arauca, Caquetá, Casanare, Cucuta, Guaviare, Meta and Putumayo

Ecuador: Provinces: Morona-Santiago, Napo, Pastaza, Sucumbios and Zamora Chinchipe

French Guiana: Saint Laurent-de-Maroni Region

Peru: Departments: Amazonas, Ancash, Ayacucho, Cusco, Huanuco, Junin, Loreto, Madre de Dios, Pasco, Puno, San Martin and Ucayali

(Source: Center for Disease Control, June 1999)

CHOLERA

Many travellers think that they are likely to contract cholera while on their journey abroad. In fact, this is highly unlikely as the majority of international travellers are reasonably careful with what they eat and drink and so the possibility of cholera infection is slight. In general, travellers would need to have grossly infected water or food before they would develop the disease. Usually, cholera-infected water is distinctly off colour. Our gastric acid protects well against the organism and a large quantity would normally have to be taken before infection occurs. There is a slightly higher risk for those taking acid-reducing preparations or those with a history of gastric surgery. One of the other most significant risks is encountered through the consumption of shellfish. This will be covered further in the chapter on food-borne disease.

Officially no country in the world requires evidence of cholera vaccination from any traveller before entry. However, unofficially many central African countries particularly will look for a stamped vaccination card. Their diligence seems to be associated somewhat more with the possibility of personal gain than with dedication to the health of their country! There are also similar reports from those travelling through some South American countries and very occasionally those travelling between India and Nepal by land.

Africa

Angola	Chad	Ghana
Benin	Comoros	Guinea
Burkina Faso	Congo	Guinea-Bissau
Burundi	Côte d'Ivoire	Kenya
Cameroon	Democratic Republic of	Liberia
Cape Verde	Congo	Madagascar
Central African Republic	Djibouti	Malawi

Mali	Sao Tomé & Príncipe	Tanzania
Mauritania	Senegal	Togo
Mozambique	Sierra Leone	Uganda
Niger	Somalia	Zambia
Nigeria	Sudan	Zimbabwe
Rwanda	Swaziland	

South America

Bolivia	Ecuador	Surinam
Brazil	French Guiana	Venezuela
Chile	Guyana	
Colombia	Peru	

Central America

Belize	Guatemala	Nicaragua
Costa Rica	Honduras	Panama
El Salvador	Mexico	

Asia

Afghanistan	India	Nepal
Bhutan	Laos	Philippines
Burma (Myanmar)	Malaysia	Sri Lanka
Cambodia	Mongolia	Vietnam
China	Myanmar (Burma)	

Middle East

Iran

(Source: Center for Disease Control, June 1999)

FIRST-AID LIST

Leaving the security of your own home to travel abroad brings certain risks and also perhaps the necessity to deal personally with health emergencies as they arise. Most times when there is a medical problem, a few simple painkillers may ease the situation, but where do you find paracetamol in the middle of the night? The answer is of course to be prepared. You should pack some simple first-aid items that you will find useful either to you or to others on your trip. The following list is itemised and contains many of the items necessary for the long-term traveller or for those planning a trekking holiday. Most short-term travellers will require only a very limited selection. The actual nature of the kit will also depend on your destination, the length of time you will be abroad and the activities in which you hope to engage. Keep it simple and do take care not to add certain items which might cause suspicion if your luggage is searched by customs officials.

Remember, however, it is only a first-aid kit, so if the situation is serious always look for qualified medical attention.

■ Suggested for short-term travellers

■ Thermometer

❏ Scissors

❏ Crêpe bandages

■ Sticking plasters

❏ Lint

❏ Cotton wool balls

❏ Savlon

■ Antiseptic ointment

❏ Savlon liquid

■ Paracetamol

■ Disprin

■ Anti-diarrhoeal tablets

■ Anti-nausea tablets

❏ Triangular bandage

❏ First-aid book

❏ Oral rehydration salts

❏ Syringes

❏ Sutures/needles/etc.

- ☐ Alcohol swabs
- ☐ Sleeping tablets
- ☐ Antihistamine tablets
- ☐ Antihistamine cream
- ■ Suntan lotion
- ☐ Burn spray
- ■ Insect repellent cream
- ■ Insect repellent coils
- ■ After-bite cream
- ■ After-sun ointment
- ☐ Antibiotics
- ☐ Tetracycline
- ☐ Cotrimoxazole
- ☐ Metronidazole
- ☐ Thrush preparation
- ☐ Anti-fungal ointment

- ☐ Dental repair kit
- ■ Water purification tablets
- ☐ Water filter pump
- ☐ Eye ointment
- ☐ Steroid ointment
- ☐ Cold sore ointment
- ☐ Safety pins
- ☐ Tweezers
- ☐ Blood sampling bottles
- ☐ Non-adhesive dressings
- ☐ Wound dressings
- ☐ Anti-inflammatory ointment
- ☐ Calamine lotion
- ☐ Hypochlorite solution
  e.g. Domestos/Milton
- ☐ Malaria standby treatment

VACCINES

Most travellers fear vaccines. The thought of needles causes even the strongest to quaver. Well, before you build up too many bad thoughts let's get one thing straight; vaccines nowadays are safe, and modern techniques mean that the fear of the visit to the vaccination centre is a relic of the past. Vaccine centres are designed to be 'user-friendly' and hurting people is definitely bad for business!

What are vaccines?

In the past the doctor may in fact have given you a small portion of the infection to help you build up your own body defences. Nowadays many of the vaccines are synthetic and so the risk of any side effects has become really small.

Ever since Edward Jenner on 14 May 1796 showed that by using a small amount of cowpox he could protect people from the killer disease smallpox, the use of vaccines has been an important force in our fight against disease. Of course not all diseases can be stopped this way but many can and the use of vaccines is a sensible precaution for the international traveller. Newer and safer vaccines are continually being developed and so travellers are able to visit remote areas of our world without many of the risks to which previous travellers were often exposed.

How do they work?

Vaccines work by stimulating our immune system to form antibodies, which are capable of fighting infectious agents. Some of the vaccines can be taken by mouth and others require an injection. The antibodies may need to be reinforced and this is done through the use of booster doses. The memory system within the body varies for different vaccines and so the booster doses are given at variable intervals, from just months to many years.

Contraindication to vaccines?

The majority of people can have vaccines without worry but there are a few special groups, which will require particular attention. You should tell the doctor before your vaccines if any of the following are true for you.

Pregnancy (or possible)

If you are pregnant or planning to become pregnant in the near future then do make sure that you explain this clearly to the doctor before any vaccines are given.

Breastfeeding

This obviously presents its own difficulties in that a small amount of the vaccine could at least in theory be passed to the child. The fact that you are breastfeeding also suggests that the child might travel with you for your journey overseas. This may be very unwise and again should be discussed in detail at an early stage.

Eczema/psoriasis

These skin conditions can be aggravated by a number of factors. Vaccines generally tend not to cause a problem but again it would be wise to spend time discussing the issues.

Sarcoidosis/Addison's/diabetes/asthma/epilepsy/AIDS

These diseases may to some extent weaken your immune system and so leave you more exposed to disease while abroad.

On any medication?

It is essential that the doctor knows what you are taking in order to make sure that no interaction might occur.

Any drug allergy? (E.g. sulphonamides/penicillin/aspirin)

If you have any significant allergy then it is always possible that you may be more likely to react to the vaccines. Again this is usually very rare but care needs to be taken.

Food allergy? (E.g. milk products, egg)

The same holds true as for the drug allergy, although egg allergy is particularly important. Those with a serious allergy to eggs may also have a reaction to certain vaccines (e.g. yellow fever, MMR, influenza). This needs to be discussed.

In close contact with sick people? (E.g. nurse, doctor, etc.)

Some of the vaccines used are given by mouth and there is a very small risk that you could infect some other person who is weakened at this time.

Side effects

There are very few significant side effects associated with the modern vaccines but bear the following in mind.

- Soreness and redness in the vaccine site
  This was more commonly seen with the older typhoid and cholera vaccines. It is unusual nowadays but does occasionally occur.

- Stiffness in the shoulder on the same side

- Flu symptoms

- Headache/skin rash
  These are very rare but can occasionally occur.

If you have any effect that you feel may be due to the vaccines ring the doctor.

Essential/recommended?

Vaccines may be compulsory for entry/exit purposes or they may be recommended for your personal protection. The requirement of vaccines for entry/exit purposes is generally a means of halting the entry of disease into the country in question. When vaccines are recommended for your own personal protection this often means that the country has the disease and you should be protected against it.

It is perhaps easiest to describe the situation with regard to those travelling from countries in western Europe to India, Thailand or Mexico.

No vaccines are essential for this trip but nevertheless for your own personal protection it would be strongly recommended that you do consider certain cover.

When to start your vaccines?

Vaccines usually take time to work effectively. For most trips of two to three weeks it is wise to attend initially for your vaccines and health brief about a month before your journey. If you plan to travel abroad for longer then it may be wise to see the doctor two or three months before departure date if at all possible.

Which vaccines?

This will depend on various factors including your itinerary, your planned activities abroad and the duration of your stay.

Description of individual vaccines

Yellow fever

This is a live vaccine, which is given on one occasion and lasts for ten years. Mosquitoes mainly in West Africa and also parts of South America transmit the disease. Travellers to Asia and the Far East will require the vaccine only if they have travelled via an infected country.

Cholera

The older vaccine provides very little protection and in 1973 WHO recommended against its use for international travel. No country officially looks for proof of cholera vaccine now.

Poliomyelitis

The risk of polio is small for most international travellers, probably less than 1/1,000,000. The disease is spread through contaminated food and also through coughing. Two different types of vaccines are used depending on whether or not a person has had previous vaccination against polio.

Polio Salk vaccine: This killed vaccine is used for the traveller who has had no previous cover against polio. It is given by a small injection, usually in the upper arm. The course of three needs to be completed over two to six months and it will then protect for approximately five years.

Polio Sabin vaccine: This is a live vaccine, which is given orally. Most younger travellers have had previous polio vaccination and therefore will require only a single sugar lump vaccine to bring back their protection for a further five years.

Typhoid

The risk of typhoid is thought to be in the region of 1/3,000 for the international traveller to the tropics — especially India. The disease is spread mainly through contaminated food but also through infected water. Two types of vaccine are usually used nowadays.

Polysaccharide vaccine: This is one of the newer typhoid vaccines. It is given once by a small injection and provides cover for three years.

Oral Ty21a vaccine: This is an oral live vaccine, which needs to be taken on alternative days for five days (day one, day three and day five). The vaccine normally gives cover for one year for most travellers but cannot be used in children under six years of age.

Rabies

This is a viral disease transmitted by the bite, lick or scratch of any infected warm-blooded animal. The disease occurs almost everywhere throughout the world and is a special risk for travellers to Africa, India and Asia who plan to trek. The vaccine is administered by a small scratch on the upper arm, which needs to be given on three occasions over a one-month period to provide cover for two to three years.

Tetanus

Tetanus is a bacterial disease found in every country throughout the world and cover against it should be considered for all travellers. The injection is a killed vaccine which is given on one occasion in the upper arm for those requiring a booster and on three occasions over six months for those not previously vaccinated. This provides cover for ten years.

Diphtheria

This is also a bacterial disease, which is mainly transmitted through coughing. The principal regions where diphtheria occurs at present are in Russia and the former Soviet Republics. Cover should also be used for those planning to live in tropical regions for extended periods. The vaccine is given in the same way as tetanus and provides cover also for about ten years.

Hepatitis B

This is a viral disease, which is transmitted in a similar fashion to the AIDS virus. Blood and sexual contact must be avoided as the disease carries a high rate of morbidity and mortality. The vaccine is often used for those travelling frequently or those who will be living abroad in regions where the risk of contact (e.g. from road accidents) is significantly higher. The vaccine is given on three occasions over two to six months and usually provides good cover against hepatitis B. Remember that *no* protection is given against AIDS.

Hepatitis A

This is another viral disease but this one is easily transmitted through infected food or contaminated water. The risk to the unprotected international traveller is thought to be approximately 1/300 to 1/500 when visiting areas in Africa, Asia, South and Central America. (Risk occurs even if only a short stay is considered while transiting through an infected region.) Some travellers will have a history of jaundice. This may have been due to hepatitis A and if so further protection may not be required. A simple blood test can confirm if antibodies are present. Protection is given in two ways.

Gamma globulin: This is a blood product which has been shown to be safe and provides excellent protection against hepatitis A — but only for a short period of time. It is given by a single injection and, depending on the dosage given, will usually give good protection for between one and five months.

Hepatitis A vaccine: This is the newer active vaccine, which provides excellent protection for a year following a single injection. A booster injection, given usually around twelve months later, will provide cover for approximately ten years.

Meningococcal meningitis

There are many forms of meningitis which can harm humans. This particular one is caused by a bacterium and commonly occurs in some of the sub-Saharan African countries and in Nepal. It may also be found in parts of Asia and South America. The vaccine is given by a small injection and gives good cover against this form of meningitis for about three years.

Japanese B encephalitis

This is a viral disease transmitted through mosquitoes. It occurs in South-East Asia. The vaccine is sometimes used for those planning to live in infected regions or those who will be exposed extensively for longer periods of time (e.g. trekking in the forests for more than a month). Two or three injections are usually given over a one-month period to provide cover.

Malaria

There is no vaccine against malaria. Tablets are used instead and should be started some time before exposure in order to build up the necessary level of protection and to make sure that they suit.

The actual schedule for your journey will need to be worked out carefully by the vaccination doctor. The doctor will be able to take into account your past medical history and the risk factors associated with this trip.

Are there alternatives to medical advice and practice?

A holistic approach to health is currently in vogue throughout the world. It is not so much a reaction against the value or effectiveness of modern medicine, as it is a reaction to the perceived dependency by medical practitioners upon technology and the consequential feeling of an impersonal approach towards an individual's health. The 'patient' replaces the 'person'. As with all other areas of medicine, alternatives are sought to vaccination, chemoprophylaxis, medications and treatments.

Nevertheless, whatever the benefits of alternative practices as regards treatment and care (and also in the areas of physical preventative products such as oils and other preparations), there are no safe alternatives to medical vaccinations or chemotherapy against major disease. Yellow fever, malaria, hepatitis, typhoid and others require modern answers in so far as immunological protection and/or treatment is concerned. But it would be equally arrogant to deny the many safe holistic practices which contribute to human health. Likewise, despite the availability of excellent treatment and preventative drugs against the major modern diseases of the world (heart disease, cancer, arthritis and respiratory disease), they are all directly related to lifestyle, diet and stress, all factors within normal human control. In general, if a traveller is comfortable with using any of the alternative approaches to health then by all means he or she should continue to use them. However, the same rules apply to the basic hygiene irrespective of where you are in the world and therefore it is essential that travellers are informed as to the safety of the products they use.

Safety includes being aware of the dangers of contracting disease from invasive alternative practices such as acupuncture, where the risks of contracting AIDS, hepatitis and other serious diseases are greatly increased in many areas throughout the world as a result of non-sterile procedures. Again the risks of taking oral medicinal preparations should be carefully weighed against the possible benefits.

Common-sense dietary factors which affect absorption and therefore the efficiency of modern drugs should always be borne in mind. Taking drugs on an empty or full stomach may cause its own problems. Even smoking or taking alcohol to excess may also affect absorption.

Apart from diet, which is very much a subjective choice, there are as many external products that claim to affect human health as there are people to buy them. As regards the prevention of insect bites, the use of creams and oils will vary throughout the world. Nevertheless take care, as generally there are far more preparations on the market than there is evidence to show their effectiveness.

Where vaccination is concerned, homoeopathy is often offered as an alternative. Certainly homoeopathy contributed much to the principles of modern medicine but again it is foolhardy to ignore the efficiency of modern vaccination practices. However, for those who choose to take homoeopathic vaccinations there is a *Handbook of Homoeopathic Alternatives to Immunisations* by Susan Curtis (Winter Press).

Given its cultural origins, homoeopathy has a wide range of products which may suit you. Some of the claimed clinical effects are interesting and include Arg. Nit. No. 1 (for fear of flying), Carbo. Veg. No. 1 (as a remedy for resuscitation), Coca No. 1 (for altitude sickness), Ledum No. 1 (remedy against puncture wounds). The one you might like best, however, is Nux Vomica No. 1 (which is reputed to cure hangovers!). Perhaps some of the most useful homoeopathic products are in the soothing and antiseptic effects of a range of ointments and creams: arnica, Urtica Urens, Calendula (the homoeopath's antiseptic) and Pyrethrum spray as an alternative to insect repellent.

Whichever product you rely on, don't forget to apply copious amounts of common sense as well!

HINTS FOR HEALTHY TRAVELLING

It will not be possible to cover every situation which might occur while you are abroad. It is, however, possible to give a brief list of hints which will be of assistance to some specific groups during their travels. In this chapter we will cover the following topics.

- Travelling while pregnant
- Travelling with children
- Travelling with diabetes
- Travelling with asthma
- Travelling with heart disease

Travelling with any of these conditions (or with children) can be frustrating and at times dangerous. Watch out for some of the more common pitfalls and allow yourself to enjoy that holiday!

Travelling while pregnant

Many concerns may go through your mind when you confirm you are pregnant but nevertheless have an overseas trip planned. Is it safe to travel? Are there extra precautions that should be taken? What about the vaccines and the malaria tablets?

If this is your first pregnancy you will need to realise that you are travelling in uncharted territory as far as you personally are concerned. In a majority of cases the pregnancy will progress with no major difficulties; after all, pregnancy is a normal physiological event, not a clinical condition! Still, travelling during these first months may expose you and your unborn child to certain risks, so precautions should be taken.

Pregnancy can be easily divided into three stages. During the first three months mothers are sometimes nauseated and travelling may make this more pronounced. During the final three months mothers will be carrying an extra load. This makes exercise more tiring and also the bladder pressure may mean more frequent trips to the loo. Airlines are not keen to have a potential delivery at 36,000 feet and so try to restrict air travel to the early stages of pregnancy. In the middle stage most pregnant women are very well and so if you really have to travel this may be the best and safest time.

Where you plan to visit may also be critically important with regard to safety while abroad. In many of the overseas holiday destinations there may be very few English-speaking doctors and it may be difficult explaining your symptoms if this does become necessary. During pregnancy the body diverts a significant amount of its blood supply to the womb, as energy is required for the developing child. Pregnant travellers may become tired more easily on mild exercise. It is essential to maintain a good fluid intake and to take sensible rest periods so that exhaustion does not occur. The pregnant traveller will also be more sensitive to temperature changes.

Immunisations and malaria prophylactic tablets may also be recommended for the itinerary in question but the general rule for pregnancy is to avoid all medication where possible and most particularly during the first three months. If vaccines are normally recommended for your proposed journey then it is essential that you discuss the risks in detail with your doctor. Usually vaccination doctors will shy away from using vaccines at any stage during pregnancy, as there is a theoretical health risk to the unborn child. With regard to international travel vaccines, although harm to the unborn child has not been reported, it is not worth the risk.

Malaria tablets will need to be prescribed if you are to enter a malaria zone. The risk to you and the baby without the correct medication may be greater than the small risks involved in taking the tablets. Usually chloroquine and proguanil are used and over the years they have consistently been shown to be safe throughout pregnancy.

What has to be accepted is the fact that there are special risks involved in travelling overseas while pregnant. It is difficult to give adequate vaccination cover and also your personal immunity against infections may be lowered. In most cases the risks to both the mother and the unborn child are too high unless the trip is essential. If you are planning a non-essential pleasure trip, think it through carefully.

Travelling with children

Certainly it is true that children can make a holiday but also some of the most harrowing experiences abroad are associated with children getting sick, having an accident, getting lost or being bitten by an animal. If you are planning a trip with young children then check out a few points first.

Is the destination suitable for children? 'Interesting' ruins are fine for a day or two but not for the entire holiday! If facilities are not provided for children then they tend to seek out their own entertainment. This may involve them wandering off away from the adults. Always make sure that children know the name of the place where you are staying. Have a family plan in case one goes missing. Attaching an identity label to your child is useful. One plan which usually works is to return to the last spot where you can remember being together. Warn your children never to wander off by themselves and never to befriend strangers.

Exploration and children go hand in hand. Just watch out for those potentially dangerous caves, holes, cliffs and street alleys.

Children have a habit of getting sick very quickly. Fortunately they seem to recover at the same speed. One of the commonest problems with holidays is that of sunburn. Children run around without their shirts and before you know it they are burnt and the next few days of your holiday will be a misery for them and for you too! Use high-factor blocking lotions and cover them up well. Using T-shirts while swimming is also useful.

Children especially love to play outside in the early hours of dusk. This is usually the worst time for mosquitoes and other biting insects. Remember to make sure that the whole family take their malaria tablets if necessary and try to keep skin covered with either clothes or insect repellent.

Encourage your children to stay away from all animals during your holiday. The risk of rabies may be quite small but you really don't want to be searching around for a hospital to stitch any nasty bite. It will be important to make sure that the kids take plenty of fluid if you are staying in a hot region. They will also lose salt in their perspiration and so this is one of the times when it is probably a good idea to let them eat salted crisps and so on. If you really do want a peaceful holiday make sure you have a sufficient supply of games and toys to keep them amused.

Travelling with diabetes

At times it may feel that because you have a condition like diabetes it is not worth the trouble or risk to undertake a foreign journey. Many opportunities to travel may be lost because you feel it is too much bother. Nonsense! All it takes is a bit of common sense and the need to follow a few basic rules.

It is vital that your diabetes is stable. If you have been recently diagnosed then check with your physician before you book your trip overseas. The doctor may suggest that you wait until your condition is well controlled for your own safety.

Before you book your destination check the availability of medical services in the area. Ask your travel vaccination centre for a list of English-speaking doctors, especially if you plan to go off the beaten track. For your journey carry all your own insulin, oral hypoglycaemics, syringes, needles, alcohol swabs and glucose-monitoring devices which you will need for the length of time you plan to stay overseas. It is essential that you carry your own medications as preparations of insulin and hypoglycaemic drugs may vary from country to country.

Store your insulin in a small thermos flask for travelling and place it, opened, in the lower part of the fridge as soon as you arrive. If there is no fridge in your bedroom ask your holiday representative. Remember that insulin will deteriorate if it is exposed to high temperatures and so do not place it in the boot of your car or in the glove compartment. Tell your tour operator about your diabetes. Make certain the information is passed on to your destination. This will help to make sure that the specific requirements of your diabetic diet will be available well in advance. Sometimes it can be very difficult to identify the calorie/sugar content of foods you have not tried before. Especially over the first few days watch what you eat, and if you are unsure of the glucose content within your diet, monitor your glucose levels more often and adjust your intake to compensate.

Before you leave make sure you have a letter from your physician, on their headed notepaper, outlining your requirements for insulin and the accompanying equipment. Keep all your medications in their original containers.

Diabetic travellers may become hypoglycaemic very rapidly. This may be due to a combination of factors such as different diet, irregular meals and more exercise. It is essential that your fellow travellers know what is happening so that they can help. Always wear a medi-alert bracelet or carry a laminated information card.

When you are travelling across time zones it is very easy to continue your medication but you may miss out on your regular meals. Know the number of time zones you will be travelling across. Travelling north to south will usually require no specific changes to your normal regime. If you are travelling east to west or west to east across more than six time zones then you will need to make adjustments. How you should alter your medication will depend on the stability of your condition and you should always ask the advice of your physician before you travel. A good tip is to leave your wristwatch set at home time for at least the first twenty-four hours. This will help you correctly adjust your insulin dosage. You could even carry a second watch!

Always carry some glucose sweets on your person in case you feel yourself entering a hypoglycaemic phase. If you feel off colour don't delay in telling someone so that they may assist if necessary.

Never fear travelling as a diabetic. Just take care.

Travelling with asthma

Like diabetics, those suffering with asthma may also fear the possibility of travelling. Again the stability of your condition and the frequency with which you need to use medication will play a large role in deciding whether or not you travel abroad.

Asthma may occur spontaneously or in association with a specific stimulus. Patients with allergies to hay, dust, insect bites or stings, dogs or cats and so on may go into an asthma attack very rapidly. If you know what tends to set off an attack then of course it is easier to protect yourself. However, if you are quite unstable and have attacks frequently, then it is likely that you will suffer in any part of the world. Patients who use medication to treat themselves on a daily basis would be regarded as unstable. Others are able to take tablets or sprays to protect themselves against asthma and may not have had an attack for many weeks or months.

Before you decide to travel, ask your doctor's advice. Note your itinerary and also if you plan to travel to higher altitudes. Have a physical check-up and make sure you are in good general shape.

Check with your travel agent about the amount of pollution and dust in the region you hope to visit. During some seasons pollution levels can be so high that asthmatic attacks can be initiated. Also, ask the tour operator about the facilities in the resort, the need for climbing steps or hills and the availability of English-speaking doctors.

Carry enough medication for your trip with you on your person, not in your suitcase. Have a letter from your doctor outlining your needs to make sure that you do not get stopped at customs checkpoints.

During your holiday don't take on too much and always treat any wheeze as soon as possible to try to make sure that it does not progress to a severe attack. If you have a significant allergy to stings or bites carry a small emergency kit with you and wear a medi-alert bracelet. Be careful while swimming and especially if you plan to scuba-dive.

Travelling with heart disease

If you have got to the point where you have decided to travel you probably do not have very severe heart disease. More than likely you have a touch of angina or a degree of hypertension. A lot depends on your exercise potential. If you get puffed easily then going on an intercontinental holiday may really be just too much. Trying to get from here to there can be tiring enough without having to worry about the suitcases and all the other items associated with international travel.

Still, if you decide you are definitely going then make sure that you are not on the top floor or in a hotel which has no lift. Ask how many steps there are from the hotel lobby to the shops or beach. Check on the temperatures and humidity at the time you will be there. Be certain that you will not have to travel to altitude. This is especially important if you are just 'stopping off' in a city like Quito in Ecuador. Quito is at 9,350 feet and even though the rest of your holiday may be down on the coast, a short stopover at such a high altitude can be potentially very dangerous. Check it out.

Carrying your medication on your person makes just as much sense for a traveller with heart disease as it does for the diabetic or asthmatic traveller. Also have a letter from your physician, know the names of English-speaking doctors in the area and don't take on too much while abroad. Coming home a physical and mental wreck is not the normal way to finish a holiday!

THE TRAVELLER'S CHECKLIST

It is always wise to make out a checklist coming up to any holiday. If you intend travelling to an area where vaccinations are required then you may need to start your checklist a few months before you travel.

There is no perfect checklist. The items mentioned here are ones which, down through the years, we have found worth while. They are not in any particular order of importance, as it would depend very much on your actual itinerary.

Check out the travel agent
Only use travel agents that have the security of being bonded. At least then you should not be stranded. Also ask your friends for their personal recommendations and make sure that you have an emergency number to contact should the need arise.

Travel insurance
Usually this is a very wise precaution for your journey. If you pay for your tickets on a major credit card there may be substantial travel insurance available but check to ensure that the cover is not valid only during the actual flight! Be certain that you are properly covered. It probably is wise to have specific travel insurance and your travel agent will be able to advise you in this regard. Remember that the insurance offered may be active only while you are abroad and may not cover any sickness following your return home.

Do you require a visa?
As the international travel population continues to grow we are now seeing that more countries are willing to issue visas at the point of entry. This is a great burden taken from your shoulders as you prepare for your trip. Nevertheless, do check in advance on country visa

requirements. Always carry a few additional passport-size photographs for each member of the party.

Do you need a passport?

Most times the answer will be yes. Even on short trips between some of the EU countries your passport is still required as identification. Carry other identification if at all possible and also remember to photocopy your documents.

If appropriate, are your children on your passport?

You tend to make this mistake only once!

When does your passport expire?

Check it NOW. For some countries your passport must remain valid for a good six months beyond your proposed date of departure. Also, some countries will look carefully to see where you have visited before. Make sure there are no diplomatic conflicts.

Do you require any vaccinations?

You can always check this by telephoning your local travel vaccination centre. The general advice given will be that if your journey takes you beyond western Europe, North America or Australia, then you may have to consider the need for vaccination.

Are malaria tablets necessary?

Once again check this out with the local travel vaccination centre. In some countries the risk may be seasonal, i.e. during the rainy season or through the summer months, tablets may be necessary. If they are required don't forget to take them for the necessary period before your exposure, during the period spent in the malaria zone and for at least a further four weeks after you leave the risk area. Remember that you may have passed through the malaria risk zone only for a short period of time, but that risk still exists!

Is suntan lotion necessary?

If yes, bring a variety of blocking factors depending on your skin type.

Are insect repellents necessary?

If there are insects, you need repellents! Stick to the better-quality ones with a high concentration (30–50%) of DEET (see p. 64), which are known to work. If you have sensitive skin make sure that you are not allergic to the brand you choose by applying a small quantity to the front of your forearm a few weeks before your journey. Remember some preparations can be corrosive to fabrics and plastics.

Do you require a travel guidebook?

Frequently you will gain a lot of very useful information from one of the many excellent guidebooks which are available.

Do you have local currency?

In many of the developing countries it is not possible to obtain their currency before you arrive. If this is the case, then bring sterling or US dollars, a small quantity in cash and the rest in traveller's cheques. Remember you can now use your credit cards and banklink cards directly at many foreign ATMs to get local currency. Some international telephone cards might also be worth considering depending on your destination.

Prescription for your glasses?

If you are 'blind' without your glasses, or lenses, make sure that you have a spare pair with you and pack the prescription in case anything goes wrong.

Check your departure date and time

Many a traveller has been caught by not realising the actual flight date and time. Again, check it NOW. Remember how long it takes to reach the airport, especially at rush hour, and plan for all possible delays. Photocopy your tickets.

Are you normally on any medications?

If you are on any medication for diabetes, epilepsy, asthma, blood pressure, the pill or in fact anything which you can not do without, then pack a sufficient supply with you to carry on your person . . . not in your suitcase!

Can you use your mobile phone?

Check to see if your mobile phone works abroad and be aware of the charges which you can incur by accessing your mobile messaging source. Don't forget your battery charger.

Pack a supply of 'holiday tablets'

One of your most memorable moments while away from home may be wishing you had packed a small quantity of tablets for nausea and the dreaded tummy bug. Don't bring too many, just enough to get you past the main symptoms.

Contact names

If you plan to travel extensively and especially off the beaten track try to get the names of the major embassies and also some of the English-speaking doctors in the areas you propose to visit.

Cancel whatever is necessary

Milk, papers, oil, coal and so on.

Inform your neighbours

Tell them you will be out of the house and ask them to keep a watch in your absence. Leave a key with someone you trust. Informing the local police station might also be a wise move.

Turn off supplies

Check the fridge, don't leave any perishables. Unplug everything, the television and radio aerials and so on. Turn off the immersion heater and the boiler. Switch on your alarm.

Make an itinerary

Make a detailed itinerary of your proposed journey and mark in any possible contact points. Give dates, airline carriers, flight numbers and flight times, hotel/hostel addresses and also telephone numbers. Make a few copies. Keep two yourself (pack one in your suitcase and keep the other handy with your passport and tickets). Give a copy to a responsible person at home just in case you need to be contacted while abroad.

Make your own list

_____   _____

_____   _____

_____   _____

_____   _____

_____   _____

_____   _____

_____   _____

_____   _____

_____   _____

_____   _____

While Abroad

*During the time you are overseas you will
probably be exposed to many possible dangers.*

*Whether or not you succumb to illness depends,
to a large extent, on you!*

*What you eat, what you drink, if you are bitten by insects,
where you swim and how much you sunbathe
— all of these are important and if you indulge to the
extreme you will almost certainly reap the 'rewards'.*

*Over the next few chapters we will try to steer you
towards the concept of healthy travelling.
Enjoy yourself of course but nevertheless take care.*

*Whether or not you follow the advice is up to you.
It is really worth while paying attention to some of
the more basic mistakes into which travellers are
prone to fall — perhaps jump might be a better word!*

JETLAG AND HOW TO COPE

How to survive air travel without really trying!

Put simply, modern jet travel can get your body to another country faster than could ever have been imagined a few decades ago. The problem is that it not only gets you there, it gets you to another time zone as well. Despite extraordinary advances, we humans still measure time by the daily rhythms of the sun in exactly the same way as our ancient ancestors did. The sun still rises in the east and sets in the west so when you travel eastwards you lose time and when you travel westwards you gain time, not only relatively speaking but literally. Noon in London is 7 a.m. in New York, while noon in New York is 5 p.m. in London. Real time is lost or gained and we have to adapt accordingly, otherwise our bodies will inform us in their own inimitable manner.

One simple way to adapt is to try to schedule flights to periods when you would naturally be asleep, for example overnight. Another method involves either maintaining sleep patterns irrespective of your new time zone or trying to fool your body through medications. Since our sleep and activity patterns are biologically programmed to our normal environment there are risks attached to disruptions.

Holidays allow you time to relax but if you are there for business then you must take precautions so that your decisions are correct. On your long-haul flight it is definitely best to avoid taking excess alcohol. Apart from the dehydration effect it reduces your ability to walk around and exercise, a definite must if you wish to avoid possible blood clots due to staying in a sitting position for a prolonged time.

Your biological clock will also tell you it is time to rest while the flight staff are arriving with dinner. After dinner it is time for more alcohol, films, radio channels, not to mention your seat companion telling you their life story! So what should the sensible traveller do?

- *Rule No. 1* — Leave your watch at the original time and try to behave as you normally would relative to your watch time. This means that if your watch says 2 a.m. then go to sleep irrespective of what is going on within the aircraft. This is especially important for diabetic travellers to allow them to adjust their medication. Never forget to check the local time frequently as otherwise you may miss some vital travel connection!

- *Rule No. 2* — Avoid excessive eating and drinking too much alcohol. Watch the smoking also.

- *Rule No. 3* — Exercise at regular intervals. The swollen ankles and feet of so many travellers are mainly due to the thin air within the cabin and the lack of exercise. Go on, twiddle those toes and exercise the muscles right up through your body. You will not find a full gym on board, so make do with what is available. This can often be done in a sitting position by flexing your muscles, stretching your arms and physically lifting yourself up and down on the seat using the armrests. Now if you think this will all look a bit strange to your travelling companions, well yes. But if a bit of exercise can help to ensure that you arrive a fitter traveller, so much the better.

- *Rule No. 4* — Take plenty of decarbonated fluids. The air conditioning in the plane and the fact that the cabin is pressurised at approximately 7,000 feet will both cause you to become dehydrated. You will need the extra fluids if you want to avoid a dull muzzy head, which is so common during long-haul flights.

- *Rule No. 5* — Take enough rest when you reach your destination. If you have travelled across many time zones your body will take time to adjust. Research has shown that it is easier to adapt to a longer day, after say a westerly flight, than a shorter day after a similar easterly flight. Indeed travellers may require up to six days to regain normal activity patterns after a six-hour easterly flight. These factors need to be taken into account when planning trips which require alertness.

So how can we adapt following long-haul air travel? One method is exposure to bright light in the new environment to facilitate the return of the natural circadian rhythm. The use of melatonin has also increased in popularity and research shows that it can be used to regulate the circadian rhythm. Your travel health doctor will advise you of its usefulness for your particular journey. However, research is still needed to ensure the safety of this hormone substance.

The general public is increasingly comfortable with the use of alternative remedies in all aspects of living and this includes the area of jet travel. Dietary measures can be effective in controlling sleep patterns. Since catecholamine levels are important for energy during the day a high dose of tyrosine in a protein-rich breakfast will provide increased energy while meals high in carbohydrates will provide sufficient tryptophan for a more relaxed evening pattern. The use of essential oils on the skin or as aromatherapy has also a proven effect on relaxation patterns.

Despite all of this your body needs to adjust and without a doubt rest after a long-haul flight is still essential. Where possible try to make sure that you do not have to return to work the day following your return.

FOOD-BORNE DISEASE

One of the great delights of foreign travel is the opportunity to savour local food cooked in its natural manner and surroundings. The excitement of delving into the unknown is nowhere more keenly felt than when you are faced with a bowl of who knows what in the middle of who knows where. Pleasure or disappointment? At times, you just can't tell until you take the first few bites. The warnings before you left home about tasting the unknown will go sailing out the window and in you jump. What will the outcome be? Well, in many cases only the next few days will really tell. Forewarned is forearmed.

What is the chance of the traveller becoming ill with a significant diarrhoeal disease? The World Health Organization would put the figure between 30 and 80 per cent. This does not mean that a third of travellers will become moribund but a large number will have their holiday plans disturbed significantly due to a dose of diarrhoea.

OK, so that's what the chances are, now how can you go about steering clear of potential food-borne dangers and yet not lessen the enjoyment of your journey? There is a fine line between the two and it is definitely a line worth following. In regard to food overseas, your motto should be 'Experiment but with great care!' So long as you are sensible (and don't forget to pack a good supply of common sense before you leave home) then your holiday can be both safe and satisfying. It is very common to hear travellers say that they are staying in five-star hotels or that they will be visiting only the better safari camps and so they expect the food to be perfect.

How can the point be got across? How can you convince people that no matter how grand the hotel may look, no matter how expensive the place is, no matter how clean the lobby staff appear, without any doubt the weakest point in the chain tends to be the kitchens. How many travellers have the opportunity to wander around the kitchens unannounced? Have you ever taken a wrong turning and suddenly arrived in the staff toilets? If so check them out!

The weakness may be either from the hygiene of the staff or from old and inefficient storage systems. The golden rule is that all food should be freshly cooked and screened from contact with flies and any unnecessary food handlers. Drinks should be light alcohol, sealed mineral waters, sodas or of course hot beverages like tea or coffee. Now don't forget that frequently in our own country food preparation and storage standards may fall well below what you might expect for others.

With apartment holidays you personally are responsible for food purchase and preparation. Food-borne risks tend to revolve around the times you eat out. However, when you arrive at the apartment it is probably a wise precaution to wash down all the work surfaces and scald the cutlery to ensure that any bugs you encounter are yours and not belonging to the previous occupants.

Remember that in a hot climate food will go off more quickly. Food preparation and good hygiene take on a more important role under these circumstances. What might have been a safe practice at home may not be at all safe in regions where the temperatures are into the high twenties constantly. Leaving a half-eaten biscuit beside your bed may be reasonable at home — in the tropics, forget it!

Right, so you have made your choice and are planning to stay in a hotel. From the brochure it looks great. The dining facilities may have been cleaned up for the photographs but they really look splendid. The bedrooms all appear to have a beautiful sea view and the beaches are not crowded, at least not at 7 a.m. when the picture was taken! So concentrating on food-borne disease, what are the risks and how can you steer a path away from the more obvious ones?

Hot food

As a good basic rule, food which is hot and fresh will be safe. The correct temperatures must have been reached and it must not have been allowed to cool in an area where contamination may have occurred. Cold meats are high-risk as they provide the ideal environment for the cultivation of many bacteria. Those of you who have done even the most basic of microbiology in school will have seen the potential for growing bugs on lukewarm or exposed cold foods.

The hot steaming meat dish will usually be fine unless the meat is really off, and that should be fairly obvious even before the first bite. Don't feel you must finish the meal just because you paid for it — you may end up paying twice! Thin slices of meat are safer as the cooking will have more of a chance to penetrate right through. Never ask for undercooked or rare meat, the risk of tapeworm infestation is too high. Certainly any part of the meat which comes still bloody should be either left on the side of your plate (and put down to experience) or returned for recooking, just make sure that you get your own meat back!

Cold food

In many areas your meat dish will be served with a side order of salad. The best advice is to push the salad to one side and leave it alone. It will certainly look really tempting but the risks are just too high. One particular risk relates to contamination occurring while the vegetables are being grown. Human excreta (night soil) is frequently used as a fertiliser and many of the more potent bugs (protozoa) will be easily transmitted in this way. The cysts of these bugs (especially amoeba and giardia) appear to soak into the lettuce leaf and simply washing in clean water may not be enough to kill them off. It is safer to soak the lettuce in a weak solution of chlorine and then wash the leaf in clean water. How many hotels do you think will go to this much trouble?

One other risk revolves around the handling of cold foods including lettuce, tomatoes, onions, peppers and so on. Contamination may occur from contact with the food handler who may have not washed their hands properly. In fact if you think about your own trips to the supermarket at home, how often do you remember choosing the best six tomatoes? Do you really think they were the best six? How did you choose? Surely you will have touched many more than the final six you chose. Even then you only got the second best six as the person before you will have taken the pick of the bunch!

Also think about it, the person who put the salad on your plate probably used their hands! If there are inadequate hygiene facilities for the staff — well tough!

Shellfish

Sampling shellfish abroad is high on the pleasure list of many travellers. Is it safe? How high is the risk? Are there no exceptions?

Again a short answer is to avoid all undercooked shellfish like the plague! They really are a regular source of trouble for the traveller and actually a risk which can easily be understood. Most shellfish rely on their filtration system to harvest their own food from the water in which they have to live. In general the bivalve shellfish (mussels, prawns, oysters and so on) live close to the shoreline. In many areas throughout the world the sewage drainage system may not be piped out far enough from the shoreline or alternatively there may be strong currents heading back towards the coast. Whatever the cause it is common that the contaminated water comes into contact with the local shellfish. The shellfish filter the water to gain nutrients for their own survival and in doing so may become contaminated with human sewage. If these shellfish are harvested for human consumption they may be transported many miles from the point of original contamination. For many shellfish dishes the meal is steamed rather than fully heated and so deep sterilisation frequently will not occur. Under these circumstances the traveller could end up eating what amounts to raw human sewage! Not a pleasant thought. The major infectious diseases which are spread in this way include typhoid, cholera, polio and hepatitis A.

Meals of lobster and crab do not tend to suffer in this manner as the dish is usually well boiled. Also fried prawns may be safe depending on the extent of the cooking.

Stir-fry meals are notorious for undercooking so again beware.

Fish meals tend to be fairly safe, as the meat is soft and easily cooked right through. Just remember in parts of the Far East raw fish dishes are a delicacy. Some of these contain parasites which may make tropical specialists salivate at the thought of making a rare enough diagnosis. Try not to allow yourself be the patient as many of these conditions are very difficult to diagnose let alone treat. Be adventurous, but always make sure your meal is well cooked.

Fruit

Many of the hotter areas of our world have an abundance of fruit, also one of the great joys of international travel. Fruits like mango, paw-paw, passion fruit, watermelon, banana and guava are among the real delights on which a foreign traveller may feast. Is there a risk? Of course. Can you minimise the risk? Definitely.

So long as your own hands are clean then basically any fruit with intact skin which you peel yourself should be safe. The danger lies in eating fruit which others have kindly peeled for you and prepared in glorious displays which would take your breath away. Remember, the more splendid the display the more the risk due to handling by the kitchen staff. If you really want to indulge yourself (and who could blame you) then burrow down to the lower levels of the display and choose the fruit which will have been protected from potential conta-mination by previous guests and staff alike. This is a bit hard on the next guest, but in the world of international health, it is everyone for themselves!

Remember to look out for flies. Filthy feet of faecal feeding flies are frequently associated with the contamination of foods. If you see many flies in the hotel, and especially in the eating areas, then really do be very suspicious of the level of hygiene. Also check the knives, forks and spoons, especially the forks, which are the hardest to clean. If you see any evidence of old food it is probably true to say that the establish-ment will not have efficient dishwashers (either the human or the machine variety). It is particularly difficult to judge if chopsticks are clean. Again be ultra-cautious.

In any part of the world, if you want to check out the level of hygiene of an establishment the best place to start is the guest toilets. If they are below standard then can you imagine the state of the staff facili-ties! If you cannot wash your hands easily before a meal when would any of the staff have last washed? If you have to stay and eat then at least make sure you have carried a small supply of moist foil-wrapped tissues and wash your hands and even the cutlery if necessary.

Dairy produce

It's hot. The sun is beating down. You're relaxed; the cares of home and business life are far away. You are thirsty and out of that half-open eye you spy the ice cream pushcart wending its way closer. You will remember being told that ice cream and dairy products may be harmful, but surely not just one small indulgence! If you decide that taking the risk is better than dying of thirst then at least follow your common sense and choose to buy from established shops and restaurants — you could at least return and complain if necessary! Choose well-wrapped items and a well-known name if possible. Never eat ice cream cones.

Even dairy produce such as cheese, butter, milk and yoghurt can all spell disaster while abroad. Again if you choose the better brands, and eat only well-sealed butter and cheese, the risks will usually be less. Yoghurt is often used to settle an upset tummy and due to its higher acid content it is thought to be safer than some of the other dairy produce. Milk needs to be pasteurised to be safe. Unpasteurised milk may spread serious diseases such as typhoid, tuberculosis and brucellosis. The UHT milk is almost always safe so long as the container is intact. It will also last for many weeks if unopened and so it is ideal for travelling.

Street vendors

They seem to pop up out of nowhere and surround the tour bus within seconds. Many will be hawking their wares in the form of material, wooden or metal animals, coins, pictures with camels or monkeys and many other items. All of these are fairly harmless so long as you realise that the price asked is about three times as high as they expect! Not so harmless are the street vendors selling food and drink. The extent of their hygiene is very limited. The food storage is poor and contamination can frequently occur even while the trolley is being packed, let alone from dirty hands selling the ice creams. If drinks are being sold then how sterile are the glasses? How are they cleaned if they are not disposable?

Pictures of street vendors feature prominently in any book or lecture on the risks facing the international traveller and for a very good reason.

They are probably one of the commonest sources of contamination and you would do well to steer clear.

Do you have to starve while abroad? Of course not.

There are many foods which you can eat, and many new tastes to try. Again any food which can be peeled, from boiled eggs to oranges, avocado to pineapple, will usually be safe.

WATER-BORNE DISEASE

Water is probably the traveller's single greatest enemy while abroad. If you treat it with the greatest of respect then there is a good chance that you will get on well together and one of the biggest health pitfalls of any holiday will be avoided.

Remember that very often the water supply may not be contaminated but it is the variation in fluoride and calcium that may cause a problem for travellers. This can occur even on the shortest break away from home and not necessarily on the tropical or intercontinental holiday. It really depends on the sensitivity of your stomach. If you are one of those unfortunates with a weak stomach then beware and take extra care. On most intercontinental or tropical holidays travellers tend to become dehydrated and it is at these times when the defences are down that almost any fluid which looks inviting may be consumed.

How much fluid do I need each day?

This depends on many factors including the ambient temperature, the humidity factor and your own degree of exertion. In general terms, in a temperate climate an adult will require between two and three litres of fluid each day for normal metabolism. This fluid comes in the form of water, tea, coffee, minerals and so on and it is also included in the moisture within the food we consume.

In a hotter climate, where you will perspire more, it is vital to maintain an adequate fluid intake. Perhaps between four and five litres may be required or even more. This also depends on the type of holiday you take. Lying beside the pool all day is somewhat different to hiking up and down the pyramids!

Don't forget you will also lose a large amount of salt in perspiration so you will need to increase your intake to maintain supplies. Your own body will keep its levels steady for as long as it can by taking salt from within the cells but after a while you begin to experience symptoms and signs of salt depletion. You may find that you become tired, irritable and perhaps develop some muscle cramps. This usually occurs in the second week. Most travellers just put this down to doing too much and so they restrict their activities — the body's own built-in safety mechanism!

Assuming that you have no serious heart trouble or history of hypertension then it may be worth while increasing the amount of salt you take in your food. Some like a glass of salt water each morning, but each to their own. Don't use salt tablets except under expert medical supervision as it is very easy to overdose.

The hotel tap water

It would be a cheek for any of us to say that all hotel tap water overseas is unsafe. In many of the major tourist areas of the world the better hotels would have a water supply that would rival ours at home. In these cases the risk from using the water will be very small. But how can you know?

Firstly, always check with the local representative for your tour company. They really don't want you sick so they tend to be ultra-cautious. However, don't forget that variations in the water supply do frequently occur and that what was safe yesterday may not be safe today.

Also you may not have a holiday rep on your freewheeling trekking holiday across the Andes or through India and Nepal. The easiest precaution is to smell the cold water supply in your room. If you can smell chlorine then it should be OK. At times you may actually smell sewage. It would not be a wise move to use this water for anything more than the most basic of tasks and that does not include brushing your teeth!

The hotel water jug

This is another cause for concern. It turns up each morning, looks clean and you are told it is filtered. Surely that should make it safe. After all, it is a five-star hotel and everything seems fine.

Our advice would be to exercise caution and not to use the water for drinking or brushing your teeth. In many hotels, if you follow the filling of the jug ritual, you will see the hotel staff walking down the corridor and using a tap which looks suspiciously like the one in your own room.

In most hotels with 100 or more bedrooms it would be too time-consuming for the staff to boil and filter for each room and so standard tap water is frequently used. In some of the better hotels a sand filtration system may be in use, but in general the extent of this filtration is so poor that many viruses and protozoan bacteria can easily escape through into the water. It is not worth the risk.

Mineral waters

Most travellers nowadays will look for mineral water and use this as their main source of water for their holiday. This is usually a very safe option and one to be encouraged. Just watch, however, that the bottle has not been opened, used and then refilled with tap water. Check the seal is intact and could not have been tampered with prior to your purchase. This also applies to soft drinks sold outdoors. Using the sparkling mineral water, or sodas, solves this problem, as when they are opened you should hear that encouraging hiss.

Minerals

If you can find cans with any of the better-known mineral names then you will be able to assuage your thirst in the pleasant knowledge that the fluids will be pure and the risk of contamination minimal. Don't forget though that the outside of the can may have been cooled from ice made of grossly contaminated water so try to use straws or at least clean the can lip off as much as possible before you indulge.

With bottles it is not quite such a safe bet. If the name on the lid does not match the name on the bottle then beware. Who knows what lies within! It is important to recognise that if the bottle and lid names are the same then this risk will not occur as the major mineral groups are scrupulously careful in ensuring that their drinks are of the highest standard.

One final word of caution with regard to bottles before we move on. If you order minerals, watch how the bottles are carried to your table. In many areas it is the custom to put fingers into the necks of the bottles to carry them to you. Not a very wise practice unless the fingers have just been through a steriliser — somewhat unlikely!

Is ice safe?

This depends on the water supply of the area. It is much safer to assume that the water is unsafe and in this case then the ice from which it has been made will also be unsafe. Freezing does not sufficiently sterilise water so as the ice melts the bacteria may contaminate your drinks. While abroad always ask for drinks without ice. If the drink is brought to your table with ice, accept it without too much fuss. If you refuse it what may happen is that the waiter will retreat around the corner, dunk his fingers into the glass, remove the ice cubes and then return with your fresh drink! Now you have potential contamination from the ice and also from the much higher risk of those fingers. Just smile sweetly, take the drink and remove the ice yourself into the ashtray. The amount of contamination from that small exposure will be negligible.

If you want to make ice yourself then use either boiled water or mineral water. These should be quite safe.

Water fountains

Travellers who use communal water fountains will almost certainly need both their head and bowels examined. The risk from previous mouths is just too high no matter how much you try to clean them.

Fruit drinks

In better hotels freshly squeezed fruit juice drinks are a great thirst quencher and a real life-saver at times. However, if you are off the beaten track and offered a fruit drink then just take care. Frequently the fruit juice will have been supplemented with tap water and perhaps some sugar. This addition of the local water may be disastrous.

Brushing your teeth

Many travellers are meticulous in watching their fluid intake and ensuring that sterility is top of their list at all times. However, they may then lapse by using the unsafe tap water for brushing their teeth. 'I'm not going to swallow it' is the usual comment. What is not understood is that any water contact in the mouth is available for absorption at a very rapid rate and significant contamination can occur very easily. If you feel that water is unsafe for drinking then don't use it for brushing your teeth either.

If you feel you just 'have' to use tap water for brushing your teeth then it is probably safer to use the hot tap as at least the water may be somewhat sterilised.

We all need water constantly. Don't forget the vast majority of your body mass is made up of water and dehydration can occur very easily in the unwary. Just watch the amount of your intake and ensure that the fluids you consume are safe and all should be well.

INSECT-BORNE DISEASE

One of the main reasons that many folks may not take an international holiday is their fear of insects. It may not be just the bite but also the severe reaction which can occur. How often have you heard someone say 'They just love me' or 'They seem to only go for me.'

With this sort of person is it worth the bother of going overseas? Would they not be better to head northwards towards the colder climates? The short answer here is no. Mosquitoes also abound in many of the colder climates and so you may be troubled no matter where you go throughout our world!

Mosquitoes are the main insect problem but there are a lot of other bloodsuckers which can also irritate, many of which are downright dangerous. The list includes sandflies, tsetse flies, ticks, fleas, bedbugs, ants and some of the larger cockroach-type insects, but more about them later.

It is worth remembering that the only reason insects take blood is that they need the nutrients either for their own development or for that of their offspring. Don't be so hard on the poor little creatures! Nevertheless they really are a nuisance and taking care to protect yourself against them is well worth while. Remember also that not all bites will cause infection. In many cases the only problem is caused by the allergic reaction to the saliva which is injected through your skin by the insect. The saliva is used to anticoagulate (thin) your blood and so make it easier for the insect to suck through its rather small feeding tube, the proboscis. Ugh!

Although most of the bloodsucking insects bite at either dusk or dawn they can bite at any time of the day. Travellers may be unsure as to what particular insect bit them. Was it a mosquito or perhaps a tsetse fly? Well, telling the difference is not really that difficult. Generally a mosquito lands and bites very quickly and just about painlessly. On the other hand a tsetse fly bite is horribly sore!

Mosquitoes

There is no doubt that mosquitoes are the biggest single worry for most travellers.

Their size and ability to squeeze through the smallest hole really does make them a menace. Many a traveller has been forced into hospital because of their severe reaction to the bite of this lowly insect.

There are hundreds of different types of mosquito and they are involved in transmitting a whole series of diseases to humans. Malaria is the best known but others include yellow fever, filariasis, dengue fever, St Louis encephalitis and Japanese B encephalitis, to name just a few. The male of the species does not bite — a truly nice little fellow! The female, on the other hand, is a ferocious feeder. Telling the difference between the male and female is not an easy task for the inexperienced and so squashing both is probably the best course of action!

In most of the major capital cities of the tropics there are few mosquitoes. The risk may be less if you stay in the city but most travellers tend to wander and so the risk increases. Especially watch out in the market places. It is worth remembering also that if you plan to play golf in any part of the tropics then you will need to take extra care. The golf courses are excellent breeding sites for mosquitoes and most ardent golfers tend to play either at close to dusk or around dawn, which is the time that mosquitoes tend to be out and about, and so there is a high risk of getting bitten.

Sandflies

These little hairy insects are about one-third the size of a mosquito and can penetrate the normal mosquito net. There are special small-mesh sandfly nets but they restrict airflow and can be quite claustrophobic. The sandfly tends to hover around your ankle and enjoys a good blood meal. You will hardly feel this little creature when it lands and feeds. Sandflies tend to be commonest out of the towns and cities in the rural areas, especially in regions where there are sand and clay banks, which make perfect homes for the preferred host, usually a member of the rodent family.

Sandflies don't like the direct sun too much and so they tend not to be a particular problem during the heat of daytime, though they can hover close to swimming pools in the shaded areas. On cloudy days, however, they emerge. One of the main diseases transmitted by the sandfly is leishmaniasis and this can affect the skin or deeper organs. Transmission occurs in most of the hotter areas of the world and it should be remembered that this includes the majority of the Mediterranean coastline. Symptoms of leishmaniasis include either slow-healing ulcers or enlargement of some of the deeper organs such as the spleen and liver. Symptoms and signs may not occur for many months after the bites.

Tsetse flies

These are a bit like overgrown house flies which bite! The tsetse lives across tropical Africa and also needs blood for its offspring. Some of the tsetse flies prefer to bite animals while others prefer human blood.

The tsetse fly is the insect that transmits sleeping sickness (trypanosomiasis) to animals and humans. This can be a very serious illness and the main early sign is an abscess or sore in the region of a bite.

In general the tsetse fly will be attracted towards darker clothing and also a moving object. One of the commonest risk times is standing in the back of a moving vehicle while viewing animals on safari in Africa. Despite this, it is true to say that very few cases of infected tsetse fly bite are seen in travellers returning from their safari holiday in Africa. Just remember that there is a risk and so take care.

Ticks

Ticks will not bite most holidaymakers on overseas trips. Those mainly at risk are the trekkers wandering through the outback regions. Ticks occur almost everywhere throughout the world and they are involved in the transmission of many exotic diseases. They really are the dirtiest creatures and you should avoid them if at all possible.

Usually transmission occurs while travellers are walking through bracken countryside or are in close contact with animals. The tick grabs onto an exposed skin surface and will commence drinking once firmly attached. It appears that many of the ticks need time to settle them-selves before they start to feed and early removal of the tick lessens the risk of potential infection. The actual time factor varies but in many cases it may be up to twenty-four hours. Don't sit watching the bug; get rid of it as soon as possible.

Never grasp any tick by its body and pull. You may just inject the body contents of the tick into yourself and probably also yank its head off, which will lead to more problems. Try to wait until you have a small tweezers, then grasp the tick by its head parts and with luck it should come free in one piece. Clean the area and then apply an antiseptic or antibiotic cream. If you are in an area where ticks are known to trans-mit infection consult a doctor and see if further therapy may be required. Some of the more frequent diseases transmitted by ticks include Lyme disease, tickbite fever and typhus. Remember that Lyme disease is the most common vector-borne disease in the United States, particularly along the east coast. Any exposure to ticks in this region can lead to this very severe disease, which can be difficult both to diagnose and to treat.

Fleas and bedbugs

If you have bites in regions of your body which are usually kept covered, such as your back or buttocks, consider the possibility of insects other than mosquitoes. Fleas and bedbugs are the commonest. Fleas are nearly always associated with animals and so see if there is a dog or cat sneaking into your room and snuggling down on your bed during the day. If so, shoot it, wring its neck or at the very least banish it from your room.

If you feel the mattress is infected with bedbugs try to place it out in the direct sunlight during the day; they are easily killed off by bright light. That night you should sleep better.

Ants, lizards and cockroaches

Again travellers seldom have problems from these creatures. Lizards and cockroaches will seldom come near you, and in fact lizards especially tend to survive by eating other smaller insects, such as mosquitoes.

They really are very useful, a bit like having your own personal body-guard, so don't try to kill them, they are trying to help you!

You will come across ants only if you are out walking and happen to stray off the beaten track. If so, you are delving into their territory and are liable to be bitten. Ant bites are more of a nuisance factor than really dangerous, that is unless you have fallen into a drunken stupor directly in the path of army ants. Not too wise!

Cockroaches may also spread infection as they wander around between animal faeces and your food.

Protection against insect bites

Almost no matter which of the insects mentioned above is involved the rules for avoiding them are very similar.

- Cover your skin where possible. Insects don't usually tend to bite through clothing; it blunts their proboscis!

- Cover the exposed areas with an insect repellent when necessary. The insect repellent usually recommended contains a substance known as diethyl toluamide or DEET for those of us who don't like long chemical names! It has been shown that a concentration of over 30 per cent is usually required to stop the insects landing. Do not use DEET near the eyes and do not overuse — high concentrations may be absorbed through the skin and can cause problems. You should not need insect repellent while sleeping at night-time, so wash it off before you retire. If there are mosquitoes in your room deal with them and seal the room from further attackers.

- If there is a mosquito net over your bed, use it. It is there for a purpose, not just for show. Make sure there are no holes and that you tuck the net under your mattress. (By the way, don't tuck the net in too well if you have a touch of Delhi belly or some such bowel illness. There is nothing worse than trying to free the well-secured net in the middle of the night as you make a dash for the loo. Under these circumstances keep it like your bowels — loose!)

- When you reach your destination buy a small can of insect repellent and squirt the centre of the room, doorframe and curtains before you leave for your evening meal. Keep the window closed and turn off the air conditioner until you return. At this stage the room should be free of insects, turn back on the air conditioner and then you can enjoy a quiet night's sleep.

- It is also wise to tuck your net under the mattress at this stage in the evening before the mosquitoes really come out.

- The electric insect repellents which heat coils are very effective and a simple way of protecting the room. Just make sure you have the correct voltage for your destination.

- If there is an air conditioner in your room make sure that it is set at a cold enough level. Some hotels will set the machine at a warmer temperature to save money but this will not provide sufficient protection. Don't set it too cold or you will wake freezing during the night!

- Electronic buzzers appear to have no effect in repelling mosquitoes.

- Always carry a small torch in case of a power failure.

What to do if bitten

As we have mentioned earlier, the main initial effect following an insect bite is related to the traveller's allergy to the saliva, which has been injected under the skin. If you can treat the bite area as soon as possible you will usually lessen the severity of the response.

- Clean the area.

- Apply a steroid/antiseptic or antihistamine cream immediately.

- Most times this will be sufficient but in some travellers there may be a case for commencing antihistamines before their exposure. Talk this through with your doctor during your initial consultation.

Summary

Basically insects are our friends! At times it may not feel this way but they keep the status quo in our environment and their wholesale destruction would not be to our benefit. Don't forget that mosquitoes pick up the malaria parasite from humans and then just pass it back again. You can't really blame them, can you?

Obviously we should be careful and try to lessen the opportunities for their feeding. Taking good care and treating any bites early will help to reduce the severity of your symptoms and allow you to enjoy your well-earned holiday.

THE RISK OF MALARIA

Malaria is usually transmitted by the bite of the infected female anopheline mosquito. The disease is rampant in many of the warmer areas of the world and travellers will frequently become exposed during their journey. The risk of malaria should not cause travellers to cancel their trip but it is common sense to understand the basics of the disease and to realise the potential ways that people may contract it.

Life cycle

The disease is caused by a small single-celled organism which invades our body. The organism is usually transmitted through the bite of a mosquito but transmission can occur by transfusion of infected blood or from an infected mother to her unborn child.

The organism is injected into the human within the mosquito's saliva and then travels very rapidly to the liver cells. It penetrates these cells and multiplies dramatically. This multiplication in the liver may take days or weeks depending on the species of malaria which is involved. After this the parasite bursts out of the liver cells and penetrates the red blood cells. The parasite again multiplies and then ruptures the cells only to invade further red blood cells. The major symptoms associated with malaria (fever, chills, sweats, body ache and so on) are linked with the destruction of the red blood cells and the release of toxic compounds into the bloodstream.

Eventually either the parasite will kill off too many red blood cells for the human to survive or the body's defences will take over for our protection.

Protecting the traveller

Much of this section is covered in the chapter on insect-borne disease but malaria tablets are also important for many as they travel to the at-risk countries. The tablets need to be taken for some time before you are exposed, continued regularly while you are at risk and maintained for at least four weeks after you leave the malarial zone. This is because of the parasite's life cycle in the liver and the possibility that the parasite may only reach the bloodstream (where the tablets work) many weeks after you were infected.

There are many different types of tablets used for malaria prophylaxis. Some of the more common ones are described later.

Note

You must remember that no tablets provide perfect protection against malaria and that the disease can occur even though you have done everything possible to protect yourself. Never forget that any unusual symptoms occurring for at least a year after your trip may be due to infection contracted abroad. You should be investigated with this in mind. Always tell your doctor about any foreign travel during the recent past.

Clinical symptoms

The only early symptom which the traveller may experience is irritation at the site of the mosquito bite. This allergic reaction may occur following any insect bite and is not specific to mosquitoes. It's worth mentioning that many travellers will not show any reaction to mosquito bites and mistakenly feel that they have not been bitten. This can be a fatal mistake if travellers do not recognise the potential for malaria transmission. We have recently seen patients back from India and Zimbabwe who both claimed that they had not been bitten while abroad. It was only when the parasites were found in the blood films that they accepted their diagnosis. Problems will commence only when the parasite starts to break down the red blood cells. This may be many weeks or even months after infection has occurred.

Signs and symptoms

Typically the patient will develop signs of a severe flu.

- Headache
- Muscular aches and pains

- Hot and cold attacks
- Severe sweating attacks

Patients may also develop a multitude of other signs and symptoms including mild jaundice, nausea, vomiting and diarrhoea and generalised weakness. In fact patients may present in many ways but the one cardinal feature is fever. Only in very exceptional cases will fever not be present.

Making a diagnosis

The only way to make a certain diagnosis is to find the parasite in the blood under the microscope. In some areas of the world it is very difficult to trust the local laboratories and so a definite diagnosis may not be available. More recently a variety of test kit cards have become available, which allow for a very accurate diagnosis to be made under limited circumstances.

Any ill patient with a fever in the tropics (or following their return home) should be suspected of having contracted malaria until proven otherwise. Blood should be taken and assessed for the presence of malaria parasites. Even before this result is available it may be necessary to commence adequate treatment. At times the parasites may not show in the blood sample even though the patient has definite malaria. This requires careful medical attention to decide on the most correct form of treatment.

Malaria standby treatment

Treating patients who just have influenza will usually cause no major harm but withholding adequate treatment from patients with malaria may have disastrous consequences.

Travellers who plan longer trips overseas or those on trekking holidays may be given a standby treatment to carry with them. This treatment dose is usually required only in exceptional circumstances when the traveller becomes very ill and no adequate medical attention is available. Always treat the possibility of malaria seriously.

In most cases the patient will have a significant fever (greater than 102° Fahrenheit) and a headache. They will also usually have shivering attacks and be sweating profusely. In these cases where there is no alternative a traveller may have to consider self-treatment. What is actually taken will depend on the prophylaxis which has originally been prescribed, and the part of the world where the condition has occurred. (Where at all possible a blood slide should be taken before commencing treatment. The slide can be stored and assessed at a later date to confirm the diagnosis retrospectively.)

The main drugs which could be used for self-treatment include chloroquine, pyrimethamine-sulphonamide, mefloquine, artemether or quinine. Halofantrine has been used extensively but due to its possibility of inducing an irregular heartbeat it is probably an unwise choice for standby treatment.

In fact each of the drugs just mentioned would need to be carefully chosen to make sure before they need to be taken that they suit the individual well.

Malaria prophylaxis

The main way to protect yourself against malaria is to avoid being bitten and every effort should be made to ensure that you remain 'bite-free'. Nevertheless your doctor may prescribe tablets to help protect you against the disease. If this is the case make certain you take them regularly in the way that they have been prescribed.

Chloroquine and proguanil

This combination still gives adequate protection for many regions of the world. Patients may experience mouth ulcers, nausea or headaches but these are usually mild. The biggest single difficulty with this combination is individual compliance with drugs which need to be taken both daily and weekly. By the way, both of them taste obnoxious.

Mefloquine

This drug has been widely used for more than a decade for travellers in many countries throughout the world. It's taken once a week and provides excellent protection against malaria in a lot of the high-risk areas. In the majority of patients the drug is easy to take with no serious side effects. However, certain travellers do experience problems which can be disturbing. It appears that alcohol may play a significant role in making some of these side effects more noticeable.

Doxycycline

This is a potent form of tetracycline and is used for malaria prophylaxis under certain circumstances. As it is an antibiotic there will be a possibility of thrush in those who are susceptible. This mainly occurs in females. Also some patients will become very sun-sensitive and so burn more easily. Nevertheless it is usually very well tolerated by the majority of patients and certainly provides excellent protection.

––––––––––––––––––

There has been a lot of concern recently with regard to malaria prophylaxis. Patients who have had reactions to some of these drugs have voiced their concerns and this has been taken up by many within the media. Unfortunately bad news is always given plenty of airtime and frequently this gives a very biased view of the situation. It is essential to remember that malaria is a very serious disease and kills many travellers each year. The vast majority of patients have no difficulties with the tablets mentioned above and so make sure that you discuss any of your concerns with the doctor in plenty of time before your trip.

It is clear that many people still decide against taking regular malaria prophylaxis while overseas. There are many reasons for this action but it is essential that each individual recognises that under these circumstances they will be putting themselves at significant risk of contracting malaria and perhaps even dying from the disease.

Some of the following are frequently used by people as 'reasons' they think it acceptable to stop their prophylaxis.

'None of the tablets gives full protection anyway!'

This is true and must not be forgotten. The very best protection on offer at present through medication gives only about 90 to 95 per cent protection cover. Because of this it is essential that all those at risk also take care to avoid mosquito bites.

'The tablets must be toxic if taken for too long'

In general taking these medications for periods up to at least five years will cause no problems for the majority of travellers. If, however, the relevant experienced medical staff feel that you may be experiencing toxic effects then they may consider altering your medication to alleviate the problem.

'Taking the tablets makes it more difficult to make the diagnosis if I do develop the disease'

Yes, this may be the case as the prophylaxis reduces the number of parasites circulating in the bloodstream. This may lead to a negative result showing on the blood film. But remember that, in general, patients should always be treated on their clinical presentation and not on the results of their blood film. Also it is the density of parasites in the blood film which causes the severity of the disease so reducing their numbers will significantly lessen the seriousness of the disease and so reduce the chance of the patient's dying! Sounds good.

'I feel rotten every time I take the tablets'

Again if this occurs you need to discuss the situation with the appropriate medical specialist and decide either to alter the way you take the tablets (with food, time of the day, away from alcohol and so on) or to consider changing to different tablets.

'I have heard too many bad stories about the tablets'

You must bear in mind the fact that malaria is a killing disease. Often patients can die within twenty-four hours of the first symptoms. Under these circumstances it is essential that you maintain a responsible attitude towards your own personal health. Just because others may experience difficulties with certain tablets does not mean you will have any problem.

'I'm getting different opinions from medically qualified personnel'

It is essential that you listen to and follow the advice of the major health authorities (WHO, CDC and so on) and not allow yourself to be swayed by individuals who may be quite inexperienced in this area of personal health care.

'I don't get bitten any more'

This is not true. What does change is the way your body reacts to the mosquito bite. As patients are frequently bitten the body usually stops reacting severely to the bite, so patients feel that they are free of risk. All that is happening is that you are becoming desensitised.

Remember the risk of contracting malaria is far greater than the risk of problems associated with the various medications used to protect against it.

SWIMMING ON HOLIDAY

One of the hallmarks of a good holiday for many people is swimming. For these travellers, taking off most of their clothes and jumping into the water seems to speak of divesting oneself of the cares of the world and getting back to nature, of casting aside the concerns of business life and of just allowing pure tranquillity to take over.

Others hate swimming. They will be busily skipping over these pages, as they are of no value to them for their particular holiday.

So if you are still here, let's continue.

The pleasures of swimming while abroad can be immense. Nevertheless there are risks and naturally care must be taken to ensure that silly and potentially dangerous mistakes are limited, if not fully avoided.

The risks are related to where you swim and the safety factors of that area.

Swimming pool

Swimming pools in many regions are clean and safe with good lifeguard cover. The risk of drowning or infection is very small but certain basic care is needed.

- Are there lifeguards on duty whenever the pool is open for swimming?

- See how clean the pool is kept. Look at the water filters. Are they clogged?

- Is the pool well chlorinated?

- Does the filter system work adequately? Can you see the bottom at the deep end?

- Is there any tree cover close to the pool to protect you from the sun?

- Are diving and jumping allowed?
- Is the perimeter of the pool excessively slippy?
- What are the changing and loo facilities like?
- Is the poolside catering hygiene adequate?

Travellers often ask questions about the risk of picking up infection from swimming pools. In general it is regarded as low and this is certainly the case if the pool is sufficiently chlorinated. Most infectious agents will be well killed off by chlorine and so transmission is not usually a problem. Nevertheless some travellers have very sensitive eyes and may develop conjunctivitis after swimming. This may be due to chemical agents (such as chlorine) or infection. In both cases using goggles and a simple eye bathing solution after your swim will usually lessen the effects. Despite even the best protection, outbreaks of various diseases can occur in association with contaminated swimming pools which look perfectly clean. Unfortunately there is little we can do in this regard unless you want to be completely paranoid during your holiday. Swimming in the children's pool or with the babies is actually a high risk. Often the nappies may be insecure and faecal contamination can easily occur.

Sea

Never underestimate the power of the sea. It is a force which at times we may not fully realise until we are taken by it, shaken about and then hopefully rescued. A truly frightening experience.

Local currents may not be at all obvious until it is too late. Look out for warning signs and never be the lone swimmer out furthermost from the shore. Swimming out to the coral reefs is a common mistake made by many travellers. The currents in these areas can come suddenly and be stronger than even the best swimmer can cope with. Get good local advice and listen to what is being said.

The sea is home to many creatures and don't forget you are invading their territory, not the other way about! Jellyfish, sharks, sea urchins, sea snakes and many others all deserve our respect.

Look out for dirt on the seashore. It may be that the local sewage drainage is inadequate and so contamination frequently occurs in the tourist swimming areas. Not a wise place to open your mouth!

On the beach look out for dogs and other animals. In some areas these animals may soil the beach and contaminate the shoreline with their parasites. Tourists can pick up some of these parasites through their skin and develop a nasty skin rash. It is wise to wear flip-flops or something similar on the beach area, especially above the high tide mark. Lie on a towel or a sunbed rather than on the sand.

Scuba-diving is becoming more popular but it is risky. Check the operators and choose the one with the best-maintained equipment and the most sensible approach. Before you undertake a dive make certain you are well prepared. If you have never dived before, stick with lessons for beginners.

If you are going out in a boat either wear a life jacket or don't go out any distance from the coast. Many stories are heard each year of crafts capsizing with tragic consequences.

Freshwater rivers and lakes

For most short-term tourists the freshwater rivers and lakes are not included on their itinerary and so this section may not count. Nevertheless those on longer journeys or those on a safari (particularly in Africa) may come across an inviting expanse of water and be tempted to have a quick dip.

Most of the risks revolve around either the chance of an exotic parasitic infection or an unexpected meeting with a hungry crocodile! By the way, have you ever met one that isn't hungry?

The main parasitic infection which may occur from swimming in freshwater rivers and lakes is schistosomiasis, also known as bilharzia after the German pathologist who first identified the parasite. This infection occurs mainly in Africa, parts of Asia and South America. Usually transmission is from freshwater contact in lakes or rivers with slow-moving water. Nevertheless any freshwater expanse in these regions may be capable of harbouring the parasite and swimming should not be encouraged.

Asking the locals is not always helpful. In general they will say it is safe and they have been swimming there for years!

The main danger spots for transmission are close to reeds and where the water is moving slowly. This does not mean that disease transmission will not occur in the centre of the river, but perhaps it is slightly safer. The only thing is how did you get to the centre?

The little parasite which is involved in schistosomiasis is released by certain species of snails and is then capable of penetrating through intact human skin to gain access to the body. Swimmers may notice an itch developing within twenty-four hours and this is one sign that they should seek medical attention. Even without this itch any traveller exposed to fresh water while in these regions should request medical attention on their return home.

Freshwater exposure can also occur while pushing your car out of a flooded river or even from simple paddling, so watch out.

Crocodiles are rather unfriendly creatures and certainly ones to avoid. There are many stories each year from tropical Africa and the Far East of people being attacked while swimming in rivers and lakes. If there is any suggestion of crocodiles in the area don't go into the water and take care close to the banks.

It might also be prudent to issue a short warning about hippos. These are usually docile creatures and look as though they would not harm a soul. Don't be fooled and steer clear of them in water. They have a very nasty bite — huge teeth! Also don't go between a hippo and its water supply. They tend to suddenly charge back to the water and unfortunately you may be in the way.

General notes

- Never swim beyond your ability.
- Never swim straight after a meal. Usually wait about two hours. What is actually happening is that as the food is passing through your stomach, blood is diverted to the intestines so that metabolism can occur. If you then exercise, the blood

supply to your muscles may be inadequate and so spasm easily occurs.

- Don't dive into any water without checking the depth. Many spinal fractures are caused by swimmers diving into shallow water and breaking their necks.

- If you have ear problems then don't dive into the pool or swim down to its depths. Keep a set of earplugs handy and use them each time you swim.

   (Oh, by the way, if you use earplugs keep your wits about you while swimming in the sea. Earplugs may stop you hearing other swimmers calling out helpful comments like 'Watch the jellyfish' or 'Shark! Shark!')

SUN EXPOSURE

*For a feeling that makes you very much alive, sensitive
to every movement of your being and aware of the
vibrations of your environment, there is nothing like
a good sunburn.*

(Reproduced in the *Reader's Digest*, May 1992 from an article by Paul Sweeney
in *The Quarterly*)

For any that have experienced the effects of a 'good sunburn' these
words will have a very special meaning. After your day in the sun you
have a shower and begin to feel the first tinges of discomfort. You look
in the mirror and admire your glow. Getting into bed that night you
remark how warm the climate is and that you may not need the sheets.
Following a fitful night's sleep you approach consciousness with
dreams of falling into a hot cauldron and tight constricting bands
encircling you. Full consciousness is greeted by the realisation that too
much sun was taken yesterday and the sure knowledge that your trip
may be ruined.

It is wise firstly to dispel the fallacy that there is any such thing as a
'good sunburn'. No sunburn can be beneficial for our skin. The sun can
be extremely strong in the tropics and the harmful ultraviolet rays are
well known to be a cause of cancer.

Does this mean that all sun exposure is banned? Must you remain
covered from head to foot, running from building to building in case
any of those beastly rays shine upon your person?

No, of course not. It is similar to many things in this life where the problems arise from overexposure, over-consumption and over-indulgence.
Life is like that, isn't it? We remain working away like little beavers for
the majority of the year, earning enough to escape into a fantasy
world, and then when we get there, we go mad. We try to soak in as

much as possible in as short a time as possible, and this includes the sun! Well, we all learn by our mistakes.

Who?

Anyone can become sunburnt, especially in the areas of our bodies which are somewhat unaccustomed to seeing the light of day in our own climate. Areas like the tops of our legs, our ankles and elbows, our necks and the tips of our ears. Don't forget the nose!

Those who tend to become more easily burnt are the fair-skinned, blond or red-haired, the office or home workers who are not working out of doors normally. Folks like these need to take special care. Even those with the darkest complexion can become burnt under the un-relenting intensity of the sun's rays if special care is not taken.

When?

The hottest time of day in any part of the world is usually between 10 a.m. and 2 p.m. During this period the sun is closest to us and the rays are more penetrating. Likewise this is the time of the day when many travellers have woken up, wandered down to the pool, or beach, and selected their spot for the day. Many would not relinquish this prime spot by leaving after a short while and so struggle on to maintain the territory they have gained by this early acquisition. Even taking a quick dip into the water is marred by the concern that your patch might be invaded. So quick in, quick out and back you go to soak up more of those rays. Such foolishness is often the cause of a spoilt holiday.

Many pools have very little shade or tree cover close by and so travellers may not realise the extent of their sun exposure because of the cooling effects of swimming. Remember also, however, that this shade may be a natural home to many insects including mosquitoes. So watch out!

Travelling in cars or buses is another time to take care. Travellers often place an elbow on the window ledge and the passing cool air may take away the realisation that the sun exposure may be intense.

Even on cloudy days it is perfectly possible to develop a significant burn. This is especially true if sporting activities are being undertaken at the same time, swimming, skiing, climbing and so on.

Where?

You may become sunburnt anywhere in the world, not just in the tropics. Travellers to the Arctic regions or to high altitude frequently become burnt due to the sun's reflection off the brilliantly white snow. In the tropics the sun is more directly overhead and so the rays tend to be more powerful but it is certainly a fact that more people become sunburnt in the subtropical regions such as Spain, Portugal, Greece and Italy than in the true tropics. Perhaps less care is taken or travellers to these regions tend to be on shorter holidays and so the rapid exposure plan is in action!

Why?

In our skin we have melanin. It is this substance which takes in the sun's rays and causes the cells to turn a darker shade, giving the appearance of a suntan. The number of melanin cells in our skin depends on the specific genetic information within each individual, which was created at the time of conception. The idea is that if sun exposure is to be more continuous and severe then more melanin is required to protect the individual. Those living in temperate regions where sun exposure is somewhat limited will have less need for the protective effects of melanin.

This is all very well but when we travel to hot regions of our world the number and the activity of our natural melanin cells may not be sufficient if we bombard our bodies with intense sunlight. Build up the exposure slowly and more cells are produced so that adequate protection occurs. Unfortunately this takes time and most of us live in a world where we demand instant satisfaction. With regard to natural protection against sunlight this is not possible. Others, who ethnically have their roots in the hotter regions of our world, have increased numbers of the melanin cells and so naturally have darker skin tones. They are more capable of coping with the sun's rays without serious damage.

Skin cancer

By this stage most travellers will have heard about how sun exposure may cause skin cancer. In some this will occur only after prolonged sun exposure but, unfortunately, in others the effects may be seen after a very limited time.

Different types of skin cancer can occur in association with sun exposure. Some are not that serious and may be dealt with simply by either surgery or radiotherapy. The cure rate for these types of cancer is very high and so perhaps travellers tend not to attach great importance to this risk.

Over the past decade or so we have seen an increasing number of skin melanomas in those who have travelled abroad or even got sunburnt at home. This type of cancer is very serious and not always curable. This is the main reason why sun exposure and the use of sunblocking creams and lotions have become big business. What is unfortunate is the fact that some travellers tend to develop malignant melanomas after only very little sun exposure. These tend to be the travellers mentioned above who are very sun-sensitive and burn easily. Also those with numerous moles are at higher risk.

What to look out for

If you fit the categories outlined above and burn easily then follow the suggestions below. Firstly, know your own body. Learn the normal appearance of any moles you may have had for years and don't get sunburnt. If any mole

- changes in colour (darker or paler)
- increases in size
- becomes itchy
- starts to bleed

make sure you have it seen to as soon as possible. This is probably as soon as you return home, if you are on a short holiday. In between times keep the area covered.

Note

It is worth remembering that any mole in a region of friction (bra strap, belt line and so on) should be seen and removed at a convenient time as a protective measure.

Protection advice

All travellers need to take care. If you burn easily then you will need to take extra precautions to make sure that your holiday is not spoilt.

- Build up your sun exposure gradually (perhaps thirty minutes extra each day).

- Don't sunbathe over the midday period.

- Use light-coloured clothing to cover up well. Darker colours attract sunlight and many insects.

- Use high-factor sunblocking agents at the early part of your trip (start with factor 15 to 25 depending on your risk, lower the factor concentration slowly only if you are sure you will not burn).

- Treat any sunburnt areas at an early stage with 'aftersun'.

- Drink plenty of fluids (not alcohol!).

- Never sunbathe after alcohol.

- If you have been blessed with a perfectly shaped head (bald) always use a hat when out of doors.

We go to the hotter areas of the world to see the sun. The sun is vital for our wellbeing but, like much else in life, too much of a good thing can be harmful.

Taking simple precautions and allowing your common sense to work will help to protect you during your time abroad.

THE RISK OF RABIES

For many travellers the fact that there may be a risk of contracting rabies during their journey comes as a complete shock.

Rabies is alive and well in most countries of the world and continues to cause far too many horrific deaths in those unfortunate enough to become infected. The international traveller most certainly needs to know about this disease and also to be able to understand clearly the basic rules for their protection.

In India approximately 30,000 cases occur each year and even in the United States there are over 8,000 animal cases reported yearly.

In our experience many travellers seem to be uninformed as to the actual risks involved and also what they should do if they feel that they have been exposed.

Where does rabies transmission occur?

It is easier to say where transmission does not occur. The only free countries throughout the world at this point in time include Ireland, Britain, Australia and New Zealand, some of the smaller island countries and parts of Scandinavia. Actually a virus very similar to the rabies one has recently been identified in Australia and so we may see the situation there changing in the near future. Elsewhere transmission of the rabies virus has occurred to humans or the virus has been identified in animal saliva.

How is rabies transmitted?

Rabies is usually transmitted through infected saliva from the bite of a warm-blooded animal. The animals most commonly involved are the dog, cat, monkey, mongoose, racoon, fox and jackal. In fact, any warm-blooded animal is capable of transmitting the disease.

Now, for goodness sake, if you are bitten by an animal don't check its temperature, just assume that it is warm-blooded!

We recognise that the bite of an infected animal is of course the main means of transmission but nevertheless you cannot afford to forget that there are other ways you could become infected. Any licking or scratching from an unknown warm-blooded animal must be treated seriously. Never encourage any animal and certainly don't feed them or go near them while they are feeding. Don't pet any animals — they are frequently full of fleas and so this is another good reason to stay clear!

Children need to be watched very carefully, as they tend to wander over towards dogs and cats and can very easily disturb the animal enough to cause a problem. Discourage your children from going anywhere near these types of animals, especially without your supervision.

Rabies can also be transmitted in another, rather unusual way. In some of the deep caves of Central and South America the bats may carry rabies and pass the virus out in their urine onto the floor. The virus may then dry into the dust and be breathed in by an unsuspecting human. No direct animal contact will have occurred and the traveller may be totally unaware of the risk to which they have been exposed. All travellers planning to visit caves in these regions should consider vaccination before their journey.

There is no doubt that dogs and cats are the two biggest animal risks to the traveller. However, any warm-blooded animal may become infected and then may not show signs of the disease for perhaps weeks. At this stage the animal is dying and is capable of transmitting the disease to others through its infected saliva. The animals present either in an excited (mad) phase or in the quieter (paralytic) stage of the disease.

In the excitable phase the animal (or the human for that matter) will be suffering from severe spasms and it will be unable to swallow. Its saliva will ooze out and it will give the appearance of 'foaming at the mouth'. Even an air breeze across its throat may set off the spasms (aerophobia), as can loud startling noises. It will also shy away from any fluid; this is known as hydrophobia — fear of water. Dogs with rabies can also be seen running around in circles biting trees, lamp-posts and car tyres and showing signs of other strange behaviour. During this excitable phase the animal may bite many people, particularly those trying to contain it. Take extra precautions at this time, as it is very easy to get bitten. In general, leave it to the local people, who are usually a lot more experienced.

In the paralytic phase the animal may just appear to be sleeping. Saliva may ooze from its mouth and it may refuse food. If it tries to walk, it may drag its legs and it appears a most pathetic creature. If it is a family pet then they may try to force-feed the animal and encourage it to take water. This is a most dangerous activity, as the family members will have very close contact with the animal's saliva. The risk of infection is extremely high. The time that this might occur for travellers is while you are staying in a small guest house or your children have befriended the house dog or cat. During your holiday the animal may become ill and your children may want to care for it at this time. Don't let them. Leave it to the owners of the animal. Encourage them not to force-feed the animal but rather to call a vet. Don't forget that not all bites from rabid animals are unprovoked. It is well reported that even though the animal may appear to have been provoked into biting it may be capable of transmitting rabies. So care is required with all animal contact.

All the symptoms which animals suffer can also be found in humans and account for the horrific symptoms and signs which occur before death. The risk of rabies must be taken seriously at all times when in an area where it is endemic.

When am I particularly at risk?

Most of the risk from rabies occurs for travellers going out from the main cities. Experience shows that the major time for exposure is when travellers are trekking or staying in small villages, though this is not to say that an animal bite in the city need not be taken seriously. Many of the dogs in the cities are very undernourished and crawling with fleas and are perfectly capable of contracting rabies. According to figures from Bombay, for instance, up to 300 deaths occur each year there. Trekking or jogging are high-risk times. This is particularly true first thing in the morning. Many of the tourist destinations around the world (temples in Asia, hotels in Mombasa and so on) are well known for their monkey populations. Many a holiday has been thoroughly spoilt through the traveller having had contact with these animals and then having to get urgent medical attention.

What should I do if bitten?

As outlined above the major risk in the transmission of rabies is from the infected saliva. So the first obvious precaution is to remove the saliva as quickly as possible to lessen the risk. Wash out the wound with plenty of fluids. Any fluid will do, just wash it out quickly. Minerals, beers, water, milk — in fact anything just to dilute the saliva and clear away as much as possible as quickly as possible.

Just because the skin may not appear punctured do not be complacent. You must still treat the contact very seriously and follow all the rules. After you have washed out the wound with copious amounts of fluids it may be worth while squeezing gently on the wound edges to see if any blood can be squeezed out easily. Never incise the wound as this may spread the infection and also the instrument may be contaminated. It is bad enough to run the risk of rabies but to add tetanus to the list is somewhat irresponsible!

After the initial washing of the wound, rewash the area with plenty of plain water. This washes away any of the soap-type compounds which may have been used, as soap can inactivate some antiseptics.

Bathe the bite area with plenty of antiseptic. Cover the wound with a clean dressing and go for medical attention.

If you are not sure where to go check with the local hospital or an English-speaking doctor. If you are completely stuck, contact one of the major embassies in your region. They will always have a contact name for good medical attention.

Nowadays we use the synthetic vaccine either to protect patients before they travel or to provide adequate vaccination cover after they have been bitten. If you are offered the older animal vaccine (the Semple vaccine given in many injections around the abdomen) try to move urgently to another centre where the newer vaccine is available.

How urgent is it to get treatment?

To some extent this depends on whether you have been vaccinated before the exposure occurred. Patients should be encouraged to seek adequate medical attention as soon as possible. Most bites occur on the lower limbs and there may be an incubation time of weeks or months before the first symptoms occur. This is the time that the virus takes to travel from the bite site to the brain. Unfortunately if the bite occurs on the upper limbs or side of the face then the incubation period may be shortened to just a few days. This is the most serious region to be bitten in and it is imperative to get urgent medical attention. Even if you have been bitten on the ankle it is important to get further vaccination cover rapidly. This may even mean putting an early end to your holiday.

Should I be vaccinated before my trip?

Obviously it is impossible to answer this question for every traveller. We have seen many patients who have lived and worked in the tropics for years without ever having encountered a rabid animal, whereas others get off the plane and are bitten within the first week.

In general a six-month rule is taken in trying to decide who should be vaccinated. Anyone planning to live for more than six months in a region where rabies occurs should consider vaccination. Also there is a signifi-cant risk for those planning to trek out of the major cities in Africa, Central and South America, India, Nepal or many of the other regions in Asia. Those planning a caving trip in South America will also risk exposure. Certainly any travellers specifically planning to have animal contact will be in a higher risk category.

The vaccine itself is simple to give, works very well, and has very few significant side effects.

Conclusion

Never disregard any bite, lick or scratch from any warm-blooded animal. Always treat them very seriously. Watch your children very carefully and discourage them from playing with any animals overseas.

Never smuggle any animal back home. The animal can appear perfectly well for months but may be harbouring the deadly rabies virus.

SNAKES, SPIDERS AND SCORPIONS

For many the fear of stumbling into a cave in the middle of their peaceful holiday only to find themselves surrounded by snakes and scorpions like Harrison Ford in *Indiana Jones and the Temple of Doom* is enough to make them forgo the pleasure of international travel. Nevertheless these risks are particularly small as long as some common-sense advice is followed.

Snakes

Snakes are found all over the world and travellers are naturally terrified of being bitten. This fear is felt not only by overseas visitors but by the locals. Death from snake-bite is, however, very uncommon and it is estimated that only 10 per cent of those bitten will die. Small comfort, you may say, especially if you happen to be one of the unfortunates. But take heart, most of these deaths are local people living in rural areas, tourists are seldom bitten. In fact you may live all your life in the tropics and never encounter a snake.

Snakes tend to avoid human contact and will quickly move away if allowed. The danger therefore is that you may not be aware of their presence and may accidentally threaten them. Accidents can be minimised by being aware of the potential hiding places (for the snake, that is!) and by carrying a torch when plodding around in the dark.

Snakes are generally grouped into four categories: no fangs (not dangerous), back fangs, front fangs and folding fangs. The venom is designed for biting and immobilising small prey and not for biting humans, so an encounter with a human often spells disaster for the snake. Most snake-bites result from an accidental encounter and they will bite quickly and then try to escape. This brief episode usually means that no venom has been injected and the risk to health is negligible. Small snakes move away when approached, larger ones depend upon camouflage and will hiss to warn you to halt (so remember to use your hearing aid where necessary). Some snakes are territorial and will defend their area, e.g. the black mamba. This dangerous snake also has a tendency to enter houses and storerooms. Pet dogs and particularly cats are excellent snake detectors. Snakes and spiders may be flushed out of their holes after heavy rains and at these times they are most numerous. As mentioned previously, most bites are not lethal and needless medical complications can be precipitated by sheer panic. The only antidote to venomous bites is a serum preparation.

The use of a tourniquet has always been controversial and is probably best avoided. Also, the practice of cutting or sucking the bite of the wound has little to offer. You may even cause tetanus or blood poisoning. The shock of being bitten alone can cause breathing difficulties and it is vital therefore for both the victim and the helper to remain calm. The vast majority of people will recover gradually from snake-bites because most bites do not inject venom; however, it is important to try to get expert help quickly and if possible to try to identify the type of snake. If the snake can be safely killed bring it along for identification purposes.

Don't forget that there are sea snakes also and although their bites are not painful their venom affects both muscle and tissue. Generally their poison is slower-acting than that of land snakes and there is usually time to get to emergency help.

Spiders

There are over thirty thousand species of spiders living at altitudes ranging from sea level to sixteen thousand feet, so it would be difficult not to encounter them at some time in your travels. All of them have venom glands but only a few are harmful to man, e.g. black widows and brown spiders. Again fear and panic after a bite are responsible for many of the related medical problems. The spider has much more to fear from you than you have from it. Be very careful putting your hand into dark hidden places. This includes under rocks, behind couches and even into your shoes!

If you are bitten, using painkillers like paracetamol and a cold compress is all that is required under most circumstances.

Scorpions

About eight hundred species of scorpions exist. Most are nocturnal, but again heavy rains can flush them out of their habitats at any time of the day or night. There are two generally poisonous types; one is relatively harmless to humans and the other may occasionally cause death. They will usually retreat rather than attack and therefore contact with humans is always accidental. The ankle beads and jingles worn by many local people in tropical rural areas around the world are designed mainly to cause noise when they are out walking so as to warn off snakes, spiders and scorpions.

Adults will seldom die following a scorpion sting but children may be badly affected. Be very careful if out late on a moonless night and always remember to carry a torch for these occasions.

PROBLEMS AT ALTITUDE

We all tend to take our living conditions and environment for granted and therefore when it comes to choosing a holiday destination we seldom consider the altitude as a factor. Altitude affects our breathing and breathing is essential for activity! One fundamental fact which needs to be recognised is that air becomes thinner at higher altitudes. This means that there is less oxygen available for the body and so we need to breathe more rapidly or deeply in order to cope. Under normal circumstances we tend to slow our activities so that our requirements are lessened but some holiday activities are strenuous and require considerable exertion, such as trekking, mountain climbing, skiing, even strenuous fun like dancing! The secret of having fun at high altitudes is being aware and taking time to acclimatise. So what are the problems? Overexertion certainly ranks high on the list. Generally you may be well able to cope with mild exertion but those suffering from heart disease, asthma (or any other respiratory condition) or even panic attacks may find that their symptoms occur more easily. The early signs of altitude sickness are commonly disregarded and there can easily be serious consequences.

The most significant problem is that the early signs may be masked by various other factors until the holidaymaker is relatively quickly overtaken by some of the serious symptoms. So, are there any precautions which should be taken before the holiday, when particularly do travellers become at risk, what are the main symptoms and signs of altitude sickness and what should be done?

Before departure

Certainly if you are planning a holiday at heights above 10,000 feet it is wise to know how your body will cope. The two main areas of the body which are affected are the cardiac and the cerebral systems. Knowing that you are in good shape is at least a start. Have a medical check and make sure that your doctor knows you intend travelling to high altitude. He or she will pay special attention to your heart, blood pressure, pulse and lungs. If these are in good shape then there is hope for you! If you have a history of significant asthma, angina, hyper-tension, diabetes or migraine, special care will need to be taken. Don't go planning a climbing holiday if you are pregnant.

If your doctor advises you against undertaking a high-altitude trip then listen to the advice. It is given for your protection.

Where and when are the risks?

As mentioned, most of the risks regarding altitude sickness occur while climbing over 10,000 feet. The symptoms and signs may be noticed even at lower levels and this is especially true if the traveller is suddenly deposited from a pressurised plane onto the ground at levels much higher than those to which they are accustomed. These can be even as low as 6,000 or 8,000 feet, especially in those getting on in years and with a history of heart disease.

One of the times when travellers can experience real problems is flying into Ecuador or Nepal and suddenly finding themselves at high altitude where the air is very thin. Their breathing becomes a bit laboured, but still they don't want to slow down the party, so on they press. Well, that traveller is aiming for trouble. Real difficulties can occur and the problems are not worth the risk.

Symptoms and signs

Symptoms are what you feel. Signs are what others can find while examining you.

In climbers the main symptoms and signs of altitude sickness include:

- Dull headache
- Tiredness and lassitude
- Shortness of breath
- Chest pains
- Difficulty in focusing

- Dizziness
- Swelling of the ankles
- Irritability
- Poor sleep pattern

Any of the above would be a cause for concern and care should be taken to deal with the situation just as soon as possible. We see many travellers planning to climb in the Himalayas, the Andes or around the Rift Valley in Africa. In many cases their preparation appears to be rather limited and certainly they frequently underestimate the potential seriousness of their actions. One recent case history may help to clarify the situation.

I flew into Kenya to connect with my flight to the Democratic Republic of Congo. The onward flight was held for a few days and so I had the opportunity to join with a group who were climbing Mount Kenya. Now it is worth noting that I'd seldom risen higher than a two-storey house and hill walking and climbing was not one of my favourite pastimes. Nevertheless I was fairly fit and a little jaunt up Mount Kenya seemed like a piece of cake. After all the others in the party didn't look any fitter!

So off we set and drove from Nairobi (approximately 6,000 feet) to the base station on the slopes of the mountain (approximately 12,000 feet). All of this took only about four hours — that in itself was quite a jump in altitude. Early the next morning the backpacks were distributed and, as I looked fitter than most, I got the heaviest, approximately 20 kilograms. I did wonder about the mild headache which had started, but, well, the air was fresh, the birds were singing and all should be well.

The next twelve hours are etched in my memory, never to be forgotten. We trekked to the next base camp at 15,000 feet. Actually, using the word 'trekked' makes it sound romantic. I think crawled might be a better description. I am not too sure why I said 'we' as by very early on in the climb I seemed to get separated from the group and spent most of the day just praying for deliverance. That night I got into my sleeping bag, I was exhausted and very aware of the dangerous situation I had placed myself in. Early the next morning the crawl back down the mountain brought glorious but slow relief.

One of the most significant facts was that this climb was not anticipated. This often happens on holidays where travellers see a bargain trip and forget the basic rules regarding going to altitude. Cardiac stress is life-threatening at any time but in mountainous terrain it's almost always fatal.

What should be done?

Firstly, once any of the symptoms or signs becomes evident don't dream of going any higher. You should wait at that altitude until you settle. Make sure you tell other members of your party how you are feeling and if settling does not appear to occur within a short period of time (perhaps an hour) then descend by at least 500 feet. Even this small descent can be life-saving and certainly the major symptoms should lessen. Return to your ascent only after you have settled fully for at least twenty-four hours. Most of the serious consequences (including death) associated with altitude sickness occur in healthy young males who don't want to appear 'weak' and so struggle on to show their prowess.

Medication may occasionally be recommended for your journey. Our advice for the standard traveller would be to try to avoid all medication where possible. Remember that all the problems associated with altitude sickness are just your body's way of telling you to slow down or provide more oxygen. Drugs tend to fool your body into being able to go on regardless.

Occasionally a drug like Acetazolamide can be used in those planning to climb to high altitude. This should be done only under medical supervision and with great care.

One of the most dangerous times is at night. If you have any symptoms tell a responsible fellow traveller before you retire. Yawning, irritability and difficulty in concentration are all significant warning signs and must be treated seriously.

One of the golden rules of being active at high altitudes is to climb high and sleep low. This means that once you reach your base camp for the night you should leave your goods there and climb for a further 500 feet or so. Wait there for a period of time and then descend back to base camp for the night. This allows your body to acclimatise more easily to the situation.

Take care with the use of painkillers while climbing. They may mask the early warning symptoms of a headache.

Conclusion

Listen to your body. It has your best interest at heart!

A Selection of Altitudes

Alice Springs	1,901 ft	570 m	Johannesburg	5,463 ft	1,639 m
Aswan	366 ft	110 m	Kampala	4,304 ft	1,291 m
Athens	351 ft	105 m	Kathmandu	4,344 ft	1,303 m
Baghdad	111 ft	33 m	Khartoum	1,279 ft	384 m
Bombay	37 ft	11 m	Lagos	10 ft	3 m
Cairo	381 ft	114 m	Lima	394 ft	118 m
Cape Town	56 ft	17 m	Livingstone	3,161 ft	948 m
Caracas	3,418 ft	1,025 m	Majorca	75 ft	22 m
Colombo	24 ft	7 m	Mexico City	7,575 ft	2,272 m
Delhi	714 ft	214 m	Nairobi	5,971 ft	1,791 m
Dodoma	3,675 ft	1,102 m	Quito	9,350 ft	2,805 m
Geneva	1,329 ft	399 m	Rio	201 ft	60 m
Hong Kong	109 ft	33 m	Singapore	33 ft	10 m
Istanbul	59 ft	18 m	Sydney	138 ft	41 m
Jerusalem	2,485 ft	745 m			

THE TREKKING HOLIDAY

For some 'holiday' means 'rest and relaxation'. For others it means pulling on the walking shoes, getting out the map and heading off into the unknown.

Trekking holidays have become more popular over the past few years. You can understand why when you look around at the pollution and hustle and bustle which surround us each day of our working lives. At times, travellers may suddenly decide to wander off the beaten track at short notice and then they usually will be ill-prepared.

Some of the commonest areas where holidaymakers undertake trekking holidays include Nepal, Thailand, India and parts of Central America. Treks in Africa tend to be mammoth affairs and many travellers each year cross large expanses of this continent. In a lot of these regions trekkers are very well catered for and so there is little difficulty in obtaining adequate supplies of food and water or good hotel/hostel accommodation. Unfortunately this is not always the case.

Before you trek

Are you really healthy enough for the trip? Do you like to walk? Have you ever walked as far as you plan to on this journey? Make sure you don't take on too much. None of this macho stuff! Just realise your own limitations, stay within the boundaries and all should be well.

During your trip

Trekkers do face some special risks and will need to take care if they are to stay well. What you eat and drink, being stung or bitten, the type of clothing you should pack, the transportation you should use are all parts of what may make up a most memorable time abroad. Let's just make sure these are good memories!

Food and water problems

Most of the major problems associated with these issues are covered in their own chapters. Nevertheless trekkers will need to watch out. Frequently after a hard day's walk almost any food or water will be thought acceptable. Your level of care will be diminished and suddenly you may find yourself facing days of illness. This is especially true when you are worn out and your own common sense may not be up to par. Consider buying a good portable water filter before you leave.

Bites and stings

If you are out walking in the rural areas it is more likely that you will be faced with mosquitoes and sandflies, snakes and scorpions, dogs and cats and a whole variety of other members of the animal kingdom. Make sure that you are well clothed and that you have a sufficient supply of insect repellent to last until you reach the next large town. The chapters on insect-borne disease, snakes and rabies cover the major points which need to be considered. Make sure you always have a good torch close by and try to stay on the main paths. Be very careful if you wander off into the bush looking for water or a place to pitch your tent. Take your time and don't walk under any overhanging trees or bushes — a favourite haunt for snakes.

Clothing

Make certain you have good boots, not forgetting to cover your ankles. This is one of the commonest ways to be bitten or stung while out walking. If you are travelling for days, have enough washable clothing. Always give clothing and bedclothes a vigorous shake. A look inside your shoes before you wear them is a good idea!

Be careful after washing your clothes. In many of the tropical areas, a rather nasty fly will, at times, lay her eggs on the damp clothing. When you next wear them the larvae may burrow under your skin. They are not particularly dangerous, but the thought of a larva under your skin is enough to turn even the strongest stomach! The solution is to hang your clothes to dry in a screened area or to iron all your clothing before you wear it. This includes socks, babies' nappies and so on. Always sleep on a raised platform and not directly on the ground. Try to set up a mosquito net if you are sleeping outside.

Swimming

For those trekking through Central Africa one of the most inviting experiences will be a quick dip in one of the major lakes or a nearby river. Obviously do take care with regard to crocodiles but don't ever forget the possibility of schistosomiasis. Many of those travelling in this region will become infected even through very minimal exposure.

Trains, boats and planes (and buses)

We have already covered jetlag resulting from long plane journeys. The physiological effect of high-speed jet travel, which brings your physical body to a new time zone before your biological clock has had time to adapt, is one of the prices we must pay for living in these modern times.

This effect is not as noticeable when travelling on long journeys by boat, train or bus. Nevertheless these modes of travel carry with them their own particular disasters and delights. The delights are self-evident — time to acclimatise, to relax, a chance to view the scenery and a better opportunity to meet the local people. The disasters include motion sickness, boredom, time delays, higher risk of accidents and food- or water-borne infections, even theft of all your worldly goods! For those travelling in developing countries, it is essential that they have their itineraries well planned in advance, if at all possible.

Boat journeys in particular are potentially very dangerous. There is the ever-present risk of overcrowded boats. Again one does not want to encourage paranoia, but forewarned is forearmed. If the boat looks unsafe or overcrowded, think about waiting for another or taking alternative transport.

Travelling long journeys by bus in the tropics can be even more hazardous. Our experiences of this mode of travel include thirty-six-hour Filipino journeys, sixteen-hour Andean nightmares and twelve-hour African versions of roadway Russian roulette. Apart from the appalling road antics of these talented tropical bus drivers (who can sleep, eat and drink at the same time as driving), the vehicles them-selves are often held together by an extraordinary range of odd parts. It is an amazing sight, and a great tribute to human ingenuity, to see how much can be packed into (and onto) a passenger bus. Whole families, and sometimes their entire house contents, accompany the bus traveller. In the absence of refrigeration, other travellers may carry fresh food like chickens, goats, pigs and other edibles — alive! On these journeys a good source of food is any fruit which can be peeled or boiled eggs and properly sealed soda for drinks. These can be bought without leaving your seat (or your luggage) through the bus window at any of the many local stops along the way.

One word of caution: thieves! One of the authors (VK) has had his trousers and coat pockets cut into while sitting in these often cramped conditions. The common denominator noted on all continents is that the thief is usually overdressed in a poncho-like garment, which presumably leaves the hands free to work on your valuables. Finally, one of the greatest health hazards encountered while travelling by local transport is the ever-present risk of infectious disease as a result of spitting, coughing, sneezing, vomit or indeed lice-borne disease from close physical contact. The best advice may be to minimise your use of local transport and to use perhaps more expensive but safer methods.

After the journey

Remember that you have been exposed to more potential illness than many 'normal' tourists have. Your very lifestyle will have placed you in a higher risk category.

Watch out for any signs and symptoms which might suggest that you have been infected.

Attend your doctor and explain that you have recently returned from abroad. Describe your living conditions while overseas.

Remember that signs and symptoms of illness may not present for days, weeks, months or, occasionally, years after your trip.

SEXUALLY TRANSMITTED DISEASE

Holidays are for enjoyment, allowing your body a time to recover from the routine pattern which has been set throughout the year. During this break, the traveller may switch off many of the built-in safety features, which are designed to keep us healthy. The whole realm of sexually borne disease is closely linked to entertainment, and this is never truer than when overseas. Defences are down, alcohol consumption is up, normal protective values disappear and opportunity arises. A very lethal combination.

There are three main groups at high risk in this regard.

The business traveller

Imagine the situation where the traveller has flown across many time zones for a four-day set of business meetings. During the first day or two jetlag causes some poor decisions. Perhaps the deal may falter, then thoughts come together, and on the final day a deal is struck to the satisfaction of everyone. Delight! The traveller will fly home on the first flight the next morning. That evening is spent enjoying a celebratory meal, some wine and a well-deserved rest. After the meal, perhaps a short walk to see the city, maybe for the first time. Into a few of the roadside bars, a few extra drinks, some rather pleasant company and, when you awake the next morning, the pleasant company you picked up the previous night may have left you with more than you wanted.

The tourist

A similar situation but, perhaps, more time is available and so the chance of more exposures. The old saying 'I can resist anything but temptation' becomes so very true. There may have been only one single 'contact' or many. Still infection could have occurred on the first occasion.

The sex tourist

Don't be fooled, this can be a male or female tourist. They go into an area with the specific intention of engaging in sexual activity while abroad. Females, actually, have a higher risk of contracting disease. This form of 'tourism' is very big business in some countries. The 'tourist' in this category will look for the younger contact, thinking the risk of HIV infection may be somewhat lower. These 'tourists' may be better prepared than those having casual contact but they are a very high-risk group, especially as they return to their own home country.

Well now, this is a problem which faces too many travellers. Was there a risk? Who to tell? What should be done?

The risk is not just from AIDS, there are other very serious diseases transmitted in this fashion, including syphilis, gonorrhoea, hepatitis B, herpes virus and many more. Condoms do not offer full protection. The quality of many condoms manufactured in developing countries may be very poor and they can easily burst at the most inopportune moment! Also they may not be easily available and may perhaps even be the wrong size!

The seriousness of this whole situation cannot be overemphasised. Don't underestimate your ability to get into significant trouble. If you have already been through a similar experience, contact your doctor and discuss the facts so that your own health, and that of those at home, may be safeguarded. Also remember that the AIDS virus can be transmitted through contaminated blood or infected needles. Don't ever have a blood transfusion unless there is no other choice. Never plan to have dentistry while in a developing country and don't have your ears pierced or acupuncture while abroad. Too high a risk.

You may remember from the chapter on food-borne disease the motto 'Experiment but with great care!' This is not applicable in the area of sexually borne disease. The risks are not worth the benefit. If there had to be a bottom line in this whole section it would basically read — 'Don't!'

Note

Some of the vaccines may be contraindicated in individuals with an altered immune status, e.g. AIDS patients or those on steroid medication. There are various possibilities open to you, but these need to be discussed in depth with your doctor.

HOW TO TREAT

In this short book, it is not possible to make each traveller into a fully qualified doctor, able to deal with every possible situation which can arise during your trip overseas.

Nevertheless, it is important that the traveller is able to recognise illness, assess its severity and commence treatment as and when necessary. Very often this early treatment will solve the problem and further intervention may not be required.

After talking to many patients who have returned from overseas we have tried to identify some of the more commonly faced problems.

Treating diarrhoea

Firstly ask yourself two basic questions:

- Is there blood present in the diarrhoea?
- Is there a high fever?
  (usually greater than 38 °C or 102 °F)

If the answer to either of these questions is yes, medical attention should always be sought as soon as possible.

If the diarrhoea seems to be a more straightforward case of 'Delhi belly' then the use of one of the common anti-diarrhoeal medications is probably all that is required. These should be used only for 'inconvenient diarrhoea'. You may ask when is diarrhoea convenient! Nevertheless mild diarrhoea should be allowed to pass from the body. Very severe diarrhoea will always mean it is essential that you be assessed medically. Inconvenient diarrhoea is when you have an essential business meeting or a long flight home! If the diarrhoea is persistent, or you are passing more than two stool motions each hour, then watch out for dehydration. This is particularly important in small children.

Take frequent small amounts of clear clean fluids. Don't gulp down large quantities of liquid. Abstain from alcohol. Perhaps give food a miss for twenty-four hours, but clear soups and a very light diet should be okay. Don't plan any coach trips until you are well back on your feet with a good amount of energy. The use of ordinary rehydration salts can be very beneficial, as this will also replace any lost salt.

If the situation does not improve within twenty-four hours seek urgent medical attention.

Treating sunburn

Sunburn is the same as a first- or second-degree burn of your skin from any other cause, e.g. electrical, boiling water. It needs to be treated in the same way and the severity will depend on the extent of the area involved.

Firstly control the pain with paracetamol. Cool the affected area with after-burn creams. Wear loose light-coloured clothing and be very careful of the regions where friction might occur. Take adequate rest, usually lying down in your hotel bedroom.

Excessive sunburn can be serious. Again, look out for dehydration and make sure that an adequate fluid supply is maintained. Patients often complain of a significant dull throbbing headache at this time. Usually paracetamol will control the major symptoms.

Lukewarm baths are marvellous at providing instant relief, that is once you can get under the water. Showers tend to be too painful, unless they are very gentle.

Be especially careful not to get sunburnt a second time in the same area. Use plenty of protective high-factor creams. Wear a wide-brimmed hat and sensible clothing.

Treating fever

Firstly you need to identify that there is actually a fever and that it is not just the ambient temperature. Use the thermometer which you should have carefully packed in your first-aid kit.

The chapter on medical attention overseas outlines some of the reasons why fever is an important sign of illness within the body. It certainly needs to be always taken seriously, especially in children.

Ensure a good intake of fluid so that dehydration is avoided. If there is any sign of neck stiffness, or a skin rash, medical attention should be sought. If you have packed antibiotics, don't take them without medical care unless the situation is very serious and no competent medical attention is available.

Travellers often feel that fever must be a sign of malaria. It is perfectly possible — if the time since exposure has been in excess of one or two weeks. Before this time, fever is frequently caused by simple colds and flu. Make sure you have packed 'your' remedy for the common cold before you leave home.

Treating diarrhoea, nausea and vomiting

This combination is a common occurrence while overseas. It seems that you are being attacked from both ends! Usually you will be able to trace the cause to that apparently mild indiscretion at a meal some hours previously.

As we have mentioned, this combination frequently leads to dehydration. Watch out for the characteristic signs and try to replace fluids as soon as possible. Don't rush them in, you'll just vomit all the more. Sipping a spoon of clean water every five minutes or so will get a large amount of fluid in without much discomfort. Even sucking a clean facecloth which has been soaked in fresh water will provide a good supply of water if it is resoaked regularly.

Anti-nausea tablets, or syrup, may also be helpful. Take them slowly and again don't gulp at it. Lie down, dim the lights, try to relax. Take slow deep breaths, in through your nose, hold it for a few seconds and then out through your mouth. Some of the acupuncture bracelets seem to offer help to many travellers.

Note

If you do require medical help, be careful about allowing the doctor to give any injection. Watch to see if the syringes and needles are in sterile wrapping. Have an injection only if there is no other alternative and if you feel everything is sterile.

The vast majority of international travellers will have no particular problems while abroad. Just think before you act!

MEDICAL ATTENTION OVERSEAS

You have read the book. You took note of the advice. You followed many of the rules. But you just could not resist that one undercooked meal of shellfish, you brushed your teeth in tap water, you ate a snack from the roadside vendor. You over-indulged in sunbathing or were unfortunate enough to have a road accident.

Whatever the reason, you are sick! You need medical attention. What should you do? Who can you ask?

If the illness is sufficiently mild, then the items you carefully packed in your first-aid kit will come in very useful at this time. You did remember to pack the first-aid kit, didn't you?

If, however, you have any of the following you will need to look for medical attention.

Significant headache, especially with neck stiffness
A pounding headache may occur in association with dehydration, altitude sickness, over-exercise, consumption of alcohol, an infection, or it may occur following an accident. Obviously meningitis is one of the particular concerns of which we are all very conscious.

Profuse diarrhoea or vomiting
Between 30 and 80 per cent of all international travellers will develop some type of diarrhoea. In a small proportion of these the diarrhoea will be significant and they will require therapy. Look for signs of dehydration, dry tongue, dry palms, thirst, sunken eyes, lethargy and muscle pains or cramps.

Diarrhoea with blood or fever
Always check any diarrhoea for the presence of blood — dysentery. This signifies a deeper infection and will always require further treatment.

Fever is also an important sign and must never be disregarded. Check it with your thermometer, don't just feel the forehead.

Skin rash

The biggest organ we have is our skin. Frequently a sign of internal disease will show in the form of a rash. If you develop a rash take a picture, it may help to make a diagnosis at a later date.

These are probably the biggest areas of concern which will drive the traveller towards finding medical attention while they are overseas.

If you have a holiday representative ask for their assistance. They do not like losing clients; it is bad for business!

If you are travelling on a less organised journey, ask for advice from the hotel or hostel management. Usually they will be very helpful and will point you towards a local doctor or the nearest hospital.

If all else fails, look for the nearest embassy or consulate. You will find that they will be slow to offer assistance unless the situation is very serious. They get so many calls from ill-prepared travellers that they really do act only as a final resort. Nevertheless, if the situation is severe, they will certainly help you out where possible.

Try to obtain the names and phone numbers of English-speaking doctors in your area, especially if you plan to wander.

If you are of the wandering type, make sure that you have an adequate first-aid kit. In many of the developing countries the locally available drugs may be out of date or may not be well prepared and so be less effective. Carry some of the more important ones for your journey as they may be of great value, either to you or the doctor, for your treatment.

In many parts of the world you will find Internet cafés. These have now sprung up even in the most unlikely locations and offer instant access to health advice. Obviously you do need to be careful as firstly it is very difficult to describe your symptoms adequately and secondly any sensible doctor will be in a position to give only the most general of advice through this means.

After You Return

*You have returned from your holiday. You had a
marvellous time. Everything ran smoothly and you
were delighted with the choice you made. You
followed the rules and stayed healthy. Hopefully
this describes your return home. If this is the case
is there anything that you should do now so that
your next trip will also run smoothly? Alternatively,
perhaps you were one of the less fortunate travellers
who just seem to get sick no matter what. Is there
anything you can do to ensure that you regain your
health as soon as possible? This section deals with
some of these issues.*

WHAT TO LOOK OUT FOR

It would be easy to become paranoid and to assume that every single cold, muscle ache or mild headache means you have come home laden with a multitude of foreign, rather nasty parasites. As we mentioned previously, the majority of international travellers will have stayed healthy while overseas, returned home and remained in perfect health following their journey. This should be where you fit in also.

Nevertheless it is wise to realise that your journey may have brought you to areas in our world where very serious illnesses may be very different to those at home. Also, the incubation time may be very long, often weeks if not months. Very occasionally years may pass before you develop significant signs or symptoms. Now remember this is rare, so relax and don't become hot and bothered! It would only make the diagnosis more difficult anyhow! So how long and what types of symptoms should you look out for following your trip?

Firstly if you are one of the very few who does feel ill after returning home, the symptoms will probably have occurred within the first few months. After this it is possible that a foreign bug is involved but it becomes less likely. The typical symptoms and signs that should encourage you to attend a doctor include:

- Fever
- Headache
- Flu symptoms
- Skin rash
- Diarrhoea
- Nausea and vomiting
- Lethargy
- Chronic fatigue syndrome
- Muscle aches and pains

Your symptoms may be unrelated to your trip but your doctor will be able to put your mind at rest in this regard. Never struggle on by yourself fighting unusual symptoms. It may be that there is a simple remedy and your doctor will be able to best advise you.

It is probably worth knowing a little bit about some of the problems which we see in those returning from overseas.

Malaria

If you have returned from one of the areas in the world where malaria is a possibility remember to look out for any signs of flu-type symptoms. Usually patients will present with fever, headaches, sweating, shivering and aches and pains. These may present days, weeks or even months after your return but it would be most common within the first number of weeks. Often patients will feel that the malaria prophylactic drugs they are taking should protect them fully against the disease. This is not the case, as we have already discussed in that chapter. However, these tablets are good, though they may modify the symptoms. If you think you possibly have malaria it is essential that you have some checks carried out to clarify the situation. Remember, after exposure fever = malaria until proved otherwise.

Bowel problems

One of the frequent problems in travellers returning from overseas is the high incidence of diarrhoea. This can be due to just a simple change in diet but viruses, bacteria and parasites all play their part. Usually if you have a temperature and feel 'toxic' then either a virus or bacteria will be the most likely cause. However, if you have bouts of diarrhoea occurring over a longer period of time then the possibility of a parasitic cause needs to be remembered. Some of the main parasites include giardia, amoeba, cryptosporidia but even schistosomiasis may present in this way. Many patients will describe good days and bad days associated with abdominal cramps and a fair degree of urgency! A general feeling of exhaustion is also common. It is essential that tests be carried out to see what is causing these symptoms and so talk this through with your own doctor.

Skin problems

The skin is the largest organ in our body and frequently the site of problems in returning travellers. These can range from cuts and bites which have not healed to a variety of fungal and parasitic causes. Basically any skin irritation which is not settling quickly should be treated with suspicion. Some of the more exciting parasitic causes include larva migrans and tissue myiasis. Larva migrans is caused by a small animal hookworm, which penetrates through the skin and wanders around causing an intensely itchy rash in the area. It isn't by any means dangerous but nevertheless can persist for many months. It typically occurs on the feet and follows walking barefoot on the beach in many of the hotter tropical regions of the world. The animal hookworm penetrates the skin of the human and then finds that it has entered the wrong host! It can't travel any deeper into the human but causes significant discomfort as it tries to find an exit point. Treatment is usually with a cream applied to the area though there are some new tablets which are very effective.

Tissue myiasis is caused by fly larvae, which are laid on your clothing as it dries. When the clothes are next worn the heat of your body causes the larvae to hatch. The larva penetrates rapidly under the skin and grows quite peacefully over the next week or so. It appears like a boil and frequently may cause massive irritation in that area. It is essential that you do not squeeze these lesions but rather cover them with a small amount of Vaseline to block the little air spicule. This encourages the larva to come to the surface so that it can be more easily expressed. The protection against the disease is to make sure that all your clothing is very well ironed before it is worn. It is particularly important to remember that any clothing you have had with you abroad may be infected. We have seen many patients returning with infection from unusual items such as pillows and sleeping bags.

Athlete's foot is much more common in a hot climate and also the groin fungal infection will be seen due to the increased amounts of heat and humidity.

Scabies is most commonly seen in those who have been working with children while abroad, but is also nowadays becoming more common in travellers who have had 'close personal contact' while abroad! Mind you, these folk are also running the risk of other diseases!

Swimmer's itch may be found in patients who have swum in some of the freshwater rivers and lakes in regions where schistosomiasis is common. It appears like insect bites and usually settles within a few days. This sign is important, as it may be the only precursor to evidence that the individual has been exposed to schistosomiasis.

Sandflies may transmit a disease called leishmaniasis. This small parasite can often be found in skin lesions which are not healing. It is more a nuisance than a serious problem but may lead to a distinct scarring in the region. Occasionally the parasites can delve more deeply into the body so do take care.

Ticks can transmit a number of diseases including typhus, relapsing fever and Lyme disease. They are found throughout the world and are most commonly encountered during the spring and summer months. Those walking through fern-type areas are particularly at risk and need to watch out.

Urinary tract difficulties

In a hot climate, with a degree of dehydration, it is common for patients to develop urinary-type symptoms. These can include frequency and cystitis and may be due to a number of causes. It is important that an adequate fluid intake is maintained while abroad but obviously any signs after you return should be investigated. Schistosomiasis (haematobium) can present with blood in the urine perhaps a year or two after you return.

Chronic fatigue syndrome

Many of our patients are seen with a feeling of distinct exhaustion, which they relate to their journey abroad. Obviously in these patients it is essential that a full series of investigations is carried out to make sure that none of the more common diseases is causing their problems. Chronic bowel parasitic disease is sometimes found and usually quite easy to deal with. Other patients present with schistosomiasis or Lyme disease and both of these conditions need to be particularly borne in mind. Other conditions like tuberculosis and brucellosis are rare but must not be forgotten.

STD risks

It is surprising how many patients present with the possibility that they have been exposed to a sexually transmitted disease while abroad. Often this is following one single contact but nevertheless it is essential that investigations be carried out to clarify the situation. Unfortunately it may be many months before these tests can be completely accurate and so the wisest course of action is always not to participate while abroad! Conditions like HIV are usually high on the patient's agenda though more commonly gonorrhoea and herpes are found. It is still relatively simple to treat gonorrhoea though of course herpes is usually a lifetime infection.

THE MEDICAL CHECK

Not every traveller will require a medical check after their journey. Usually the traveller will have symptoms and this will have sent them in the direction of their doctor. Some, however, will have nothing wrong with them and yet will benefit from a post-exposure medical check-up. These generally are travellers who have lived overseas for a longer period of time or those who know they have been exposed to disease while abroad. This typically includes those who have been trekking.

The doctor will need to know the answers to various questions:

- Where were you while abroad?
- For how long did you take your malaria prophylaxis if required?
- What vaccines did you have before your journey?
- How many were in your party? Were others sick?
- Did you eat local foods? What types specifically?
- Did you use tap water?
- Where did you swim?
- Did you get sunburnt?
- Did mosquitoes bite you?
- Did any other insects bite you?
- Were you bitten by a dog, a cat, a monkey, etc.?

After this background information your doctor will review your time abroad. You will need to relate any episode of illness which may have occurred, and what was done about it. Did you have medical attention? What did it involve? Your past medical history, along with that of your family, will be briefly reviewed. Your doctor will then want to examine you for any signs of swollen glands, chest infection, enlargement of the liver or spleen, along with various other specific tests depending on your actual history. Following this, the doctor will probably request various investigations. This will frequently include a blood screen and also tests of your stool and urine. Even if you have no symptoms these are worth while.

In our experience up to 30 per cent of long-term travellers have evidence of being exposed to parasites. The vast majority are harmless and will require no treatment.

It is vital to realise that even though you have had a full post-exposure medical screen with the doctor, you still can develop signs and symptoms even for the first time some months later. This would be unusual, but possible. Just remember to keep an open mind and don't forget that you have been abroad.

YOUR NEXT TRIP

Most international travellers continue to travel. Once you have experienced the real joys involved in seeing new countries, experiencing different cultures with their various cuisines and meeting and making friends, it is difficult not to travel again.

You have been bitten by the 'travel bug'. This is usually a lifelong infection! Life may never be the same again. Certainly as you sit looking out on a bleak winter dawn you will have memories which will last for a lifetime.

So, accepting that you probably will venture abroad in the future, should you do anything at this stage to prepare? Yes. Some simple actions now will save hours of frustration and heartache in the future.

Safely pack away your passport and vaccination card. Choose a place where you will remember them for your next journey. Check the expiry date of your passport, and if necessary, make a note in your diary to renew it in plenty of time. Before you hide away your vaccination card, check if you were advised to have a final vaccine after your trip. This is very common if there was not sufficient time before this current journey. If you do need a final vaccination, note the date and make an appointment.

Sort out your foreign money. Keep the various currencies separate but in the same general area.

Make notes on what you enjoyed, and also what went wrong on this trip. Put the list with your travel documents and plan to review it before you book your next holiday. Give marks out of ten to the travel agency, the resort, the time of year and possibly even your travelling companions!

If you have taken photos get them developed soon. Mount them in an album and put short comments under each one. This is a whole lot more fun for your visitors and will also help to remind you of your trip.

Appendices
Travel in Health

NORTHERN AFRICA

Common destinations: Morocco, Tunisia and Egypt

Typical tourist vaccines: typhoid, poliomyelitis, tetanus and hepatitis A

Many travellers will be aiming towards some of the Northern African coastline for their holiday. These are areas where the weather is usually quite predictably hot and dry and so sometimes the level of food hygiene can be low. Take special care where you eat and avoid food that you think might have been reheated.

The mosquito-borne diseases are quite rare and the majority of travellers will not need to take any malaria tablets. There are a few small exceptions to this rule so check it out before you travel. Nevertheless despite the lack of malaria other diseases can be transmitted through the bite of mosquitoes and sandflies. Use plenty of insect repellent when necessary and cover those arms and legs, especially in the evening.

Rabies is present throughout the area so avoid feeding or getting too close to any dogs or cats. By the way, camels could also transmit rabies though this would be somewhat unfortunate!

Jumping into the Nile for a swim is probably most unwise as apart from the pollution there may be a risk of schistosomiasis in some areas.

During the summer months the temperatures in this region can be very high and a bad dose of sunburn can certainly spoil a holiday. Watch those young children particularly.

SUB-SAHARAN AFRICA

Common destinations: Gambia, Ghana, Kenya, Malawi, Mauritius, Nigeria, Seychelles, Tanzania, Zambia and Zimbabwe

Typical tourist vaccines: yellow fever, typhoid, poliomyelitis, tetanus and hepatitis A

Tourists will frequently head for either Gambia on the west coast of central Africa or perhaps Kenya/Tanzania on the east. Others will be meandering across Africa on some form of trans-Africa safari. Both groups will need to take special care with their health. The main risk which will spring to most people's minds is malaria. This is certainly the one that causes most anguish and despair, both when deciding whether or not to take malaria tablets (and if so which one to take) and worrying about actually getting the disease. The answer is quite simple in many ways — just remember malaria can easily kill! That should help to clarify your thoughts when trying to make decisions. It is essential that all those planning to travel to these regions discuss this whole situation at length with their vaccinating doctor in plenty of time before their trip. Don't be unfairly swayed by friends, think logically and make an informed decision, remembering the potential severity of the condition. Mauritius and the Seychelles are the countries in this list which are exceptions in that a malaria risk does not occur.

Visiting Victoria Falls is a common plan for many in this region. The sight is spectacular but don't forget this is one of the highest-risk regions for malaria in the world (during the rainy season — mainly October to March) and don't even consider going off the bungee jump even if it is reputed to be one of the world's highest!

A lot of the other advice for central Africa will be the same as for the northern part of the continent. Just also remember the really significant risk of schistosomiasis if you go swimming or walking through any fresh water in this region. This rotten disease can present in a multitude of ways and cause a miserable illness. Treatment is simple though in many cases the diagnosis can be delayed for a long time until the disease is considered.

Many of our travellers to these regions may need to think about some of the extra vaccines if they will be off the beaten track or wandering for a more prolonged time. These will include vaccines against meningitis, diphtheria, hepatitis B and rabies. Some time may be needed for the course to be completed so check in early.

SOUTHERN AFRICA

Common destinations: Botswana, Lesotho, Namibia, South Africa and Swaziland

Typical tourist vaccines: typhoid, poliomyelitis, tetanus and hepatitis A

The security risks in Johannesburg have worried people over many years but the majority of tourists experience no difficulties. Certainly the rest of the country seems fine and the reports of disturbances in these regions are no more common than in almost any other tourist destination throughout the world. Many hire a car in Cape Town and head towards Port Elizabeth along the Garden Route. This is a beautiful route but take care as you drive along. Give way to everyone and drive at a sensible rate. If you become tired or dehydrated stop and have a break. Just watch where and what you eat, remembering that streetside vendors are best avoided!

The only malaria risks in these regions are in northern Namibia and Botswana in the Okavango region or over in the Kruger National Park on the border with Mozambique. If you are unsure of your itinerary check it out with your travel agent and then your vaccinating doctor to make sure one way or the other. Nevertheless mosquitoes are common so take care to cover up well in the evenings and use good insect repellent.

If you go off playing golf on any of the excellent courses take special care to stay out of the rough! This will improve your score but also keep you clear of the risks from snakes, scorpions and even ticks that may be lurking in the undergrowth.

NORTH AMERICA

Common destinations: Bermuda, Canada and USA

Typical tourist vaccines: usually none, though this depends on itinerary

Generally the health risks while travelling in these regions are very similar to those at home. Car accidents occur far too commonly with tourists who forget on which side of the road they should be driving so take care! Extremes of temperature are found throughout the year so be prepared. During the hotter summer months you should try to take care with food and water hygiene once you are outside the major cities.

If you plan to go trekking or walking in any rural areas then be aware that Lyme disease (transmitted by ticks) occurs very commonly. If you find that you will be wandering through long grass, bushes or the like, cover up with long trousers and use insect repellent on any exposed areas. After your walk do a 'tick search' and especially look in all those odd places like the groin and axilla (armpit). Remember that rabies occurs in this region so avoid petting any animals.

Remember that reports from the United States quite often tell of tourists who have been held at gunpoint and robbed. Just be careful about offering lifts to strangers or being alone in an isolated area.

CENTRAL AMERICA

Common destinations: Belize, El Salvador, Guatemala, Honduras, Mexico, Nicaragua and Panama

Typical tourist vaccines: typhoid, tetanus, hepatitis A (and yellow fever for Panama)

The level of food and water hygiene in Central America is quite low. Certainly you should avoid food from open market stalls unless it is fruit that you are going to peel yourself. Really nasty diseases like amoebiasis, bacillary dysentery and typhoid occur commonly in the region so make sure all food is well cooked and that the water you drink is either correctly bottled or recently boiled.

Rabies is widespread throughout the region so avoid petting any dogs or cats particularly but remember that any warm-blooded animal may transmit the disease. Snakes may be a hazard in some areas so watch where you sit and walk. If you are out in the desert areas try to be careful where you step and also before you lift any rock.

A recent problem has been from a mosquito-borne disease called dengue fever. This viral disease has been found in Central America over the past years and it can cause a lot of sickness. Try to avoid the mosquito bites (probably quite wise anyhow) by using good insect repellent and covering up properly. The mosquitoes that are involved in this disease tend to bite during the day so take care at all times. Remember that malaria does also occur throughout this region so prophylaxis will usually be required.

CARIBBEAN REGION

Common destinations: Antigua and Barbuda, Bahamas, Barbados, Virgin Islands, Cayman Islands, Cuba, Dominican Republic, Grenada, Jamaica, St Kitts and Nevis, St Lucia, Trinidad and Tobago

Typical tourist vaccines: typhoid, poliomyelitis, tetanus and hepatitis A

This group of islands usually has a great climate throughout the year but they are in the hurricane zone. Heavy winds and high rainfall can occur so check out the expected climate before you leave home!

Malaria does not occur in any of the islands except Haiti and the Dominican Republic. Nevertheless mosquitoes can abound and dengue fever can cause quite a bit of sickness. Cover up and use good insect repellent.

Take care swimming in the sea as strong currents can suddenly spring up and cause even the most experienced swimmer problems. Also watch out for sunburn, which can easily ruin a holiday. Children are at particular risk so it is often a good idea for them to wear a light T-shirt while swimming. If walking along the beaches above the high tide mark it will be worth while wearing a pair of flip-flops to avoid a rather unpleasant disease called larva migrans. This little larva can get in under the skin and then wander about the place causing a horrible itchy rash. It is simple enough to cure but often patients don't turn up for treatment until they have been really demented by the itch.

Other problems in this region involve spiny sea urchins and jellyfish. Some swimmers may have nasty cuts or stings from the coral reef. It is also worth remembering that rabies can occur on some of the islands. One of the main animals involved is the mongoose so take care if you see a mad one heading your direction!

TROPICAL SOUTH AMERICA

Common destinations: Bolivia, Brazil, Colombia, Ecuador, Peru and Venezuela

Typical tourist vaccines: yellow fever, typhoid, tetanus and hepatitis A

This is a very diffuse region with colossal changes in climate depending on your itinerary. Both the main malaria and yellow fever risks occur in the Amazon region and this may be included in the plans of those visiting parts of Brazil, Bolivia, Colombia or Venezuela. Nevertheless yellow fever vaccine is usually given to all as the authorities may insist on it depending on your itinerary.

Food and water hygiene is not always perfect so obey the usual common-sense rules and don't be tempted to eat food from street vendors no matter how appetising it may look or no matter how hungry you may be!

In areas like Machu Picchu it is also important to try to avoid the sandflies which will be buzzing about the place. If this is on your travel plan then make sure that you have plenty of insect repellent and that day wear long trousers or slacks. It may be somewhat hot but the protection against the bites will be worth its weight in gold! If you are planning this type of trekking trip remember that you will be travelling up to a reasonable altitude so take your time and be sensible. Even when arriving into Quito (Ecuador) the 9,000-foot altitude can knock the wind from your sails. This is particularly true for the older traveller so slow down for the first day or so and allow nature do its work.

Wandering about in these regions may also put you at risk from rabies so avoid dogs, cats, monkeys and anything else which may look mad! Leeches can also latch on if you insist on wading through some of the swampy regions but then if that is what you are into you probably need your head examined anyhow!

Those planning to visit the Galapagos Islands should take along plenty of sunblock as many tourists return from this trip doing a very good impersonation of an embarrassed lobster.

Security is a factor in many of these South American countries so be careful where you go and don't take unnecessary risks.

TEMPERATE SOUTH AMERICA

Common destinations: Argentina, Chile and Uruguay

Typical tourist vaccines: typhoid, tetanus and hepatitis A

Malaria is just about non-existent in this region. There is a very small exception towards the northern part of Argentina but this is a region tourists seldom visit. Other bug-biting diseases can occur so cover up and use sensible insect repellent when necessary.

A good amount of gastroenteritis can occur in the unwary traveller who has forgotten the usual rules regarding what you should eat and drink. Nevertheless with a bit of care and a lot of common sense this should not be a problem. It is always a wise choice to make sure any meat is very well cooked to reduce the chance of tapeworm and it is also worth remembering that outbreaks of cholera due to contaminated water supply have been reported at times.

Hepatitis A occurs in many regions of the world and this region is no exception. The coastal regions tend to have more than their share of bowel parasitic diseases so keep your guard up at all times.

EAST ASIA

Common destinations: China, Hong Kong, Korea and Japan

Typical tourist vaccines: typhoid, poliomyelitis, tetanus and hepatitis A

Within this region there are vast cities, high mountain ranges, deserts and subtropical forests. This is quite a variety of terrains and for this reason it is hard to identify specific health risks. These will depend a lot on your choice of itinerary. While the only significant difficulties caused by business trips to major cities may be those associated with jetlag, the person trekking throughout the region could be exposed to many different types of health problem.

Hepatitis is a common problem throughout East Asia. This includes hepatitis A and E (food- and water-borne) and hepatitis B (sexually and blood-borne). Obviously, eating food from street vendors is a risky business and should be avoided. There is a wide variety of nasty parasitic diseases transmitted by eating undercooked fish or snails/slugs. Again, for short trips, not worth the risk!

Rabies occurs throughout the region and it is essential to avoid all contact with possibly infected animals. The availability of the newer synthetic rabies vaccine is variable and often the older animal variety (Semple vaccine) may be offered to those bitten. Schistosomiasis (bilharzia) is found in the Yangtze Kiang river of China. Poliomyelitis is rare but brucellosis can occur so avoid unpasteurised milk.

EASTERN SOUTH ASIA

Common destinations: Brunei, Darussalam, Cambodia, Indonesia, Laos, Malaysia, Philippines, Singapore, Thailand and Vietnam

Typical tourist vaccines: typhoid, poliomyelitis, tetanus and hepatitis A

Food- and water-borne diseases are common throughout the region. Outbreaks of cholera, amoebic and bacillary dysentery, typhoid and hepatitis (A and E) may all occur. Nevertheless the careful traveller has little cause for concern. Watch what you eat, stick with the freshly cooked foods, avoid the cold salads and never eat shellfish.

The number of mosquitoes present will depend on the time of the year as this region has a distinct monsoon season. During these months (usually April to October) the risk of being bitten by mosquitoes increases considerably. In the regions where malaria transmission occurs this is a serious problem as the level of resistance to the main drugs used for protection is very high. Nevertheless, for most visitors who stay within the main tourist centres, the risk of malaria is small and prophylaxis may not even be required.

Schistosomiasis occurs in the rural parts of the southern Philippines and in central Sulawesi (Indonesia) and also in a small area of the Mekong delta in Vietnam. A small amount of poliomyelitis remains in the Mekong delta and in southern Vietnam.

Snakes, leeches and rabies all occur. Wandering through flooded rivers is rather unwise, as leptospirosis (Weil's disease, rat-bite fever) is also a risk factor in this region.

MIDDLE SOUTH ASIA

Common destinations: Bangladesh, India, Maldives, Nepal, Pakistan and Sri Lanka

Typical tourist vaccines: typhoid, poliomyelitis, tetanus and hepatitis A

This colossal region covers many different countries where, because of the extreme range of geographical terrains, the risk of different diseases is considerable. Cholera outbreaks are frequently reported (especially after flooding or after major population movements associated with war or natural disaster). Dysentery (amoebic and bacillary) is common and large epidemics of hepatitis E can occur. Brucellosis may be contracted through drinking unpasteurised milk.

Outbreaks of meningococcal meningitis are often reported throughout the region (mainly India and Nepal) and poliomyelitis eradication programmes are under way to control the disease. A very small focus of schistosomiasis persists in south-western Iran. Snakes and rabies occur throughout most of the countries in the area.

A great variety of biting insects transmits disease throughout the region. Mosquitoes carry both malaria and filariasis in Bangladesh, India and parts of Sri Lanka. Malaria transmission also occurs in Armenia, Azerbaijan and Tajikistan though the risks are small. However, in India this is not the case as the disease risk has increased considerably over the past decade. Sandflies also may cause trouble and may transmit a disease called leishmaniasis (Afghanistan, Azerbaijan, Bangladesh, India, Iran, Pakistan, Tajikistan), and a number of tick-borne diseases are also reported (Afghanistan, India, Iran). Dengue fever and Japanese B encephalitis (both transmitted by mosquitoes) have been seen mainly in the eastern part of this region.

135

WESTERN SOUTH ASIA

Common destinations: Bahrain, Cyprus, Israel, Jordan, Kuwait, Lebanon, Oman, Saudi Arabia, Syria and Turkey

Typical tourist vaccines: typhoid, poliomyelitis, tetanus and hepatitis A

This is the region often referred to as the Middle East. Generally the risks to tourists are quite small.

Typhoid and hepatitis A are found throughout the region and tape-worm infection (taeniasis, from undercooked infected beef, pork and fish) occurs. Brucellosis is found and may cause considerable difficulty for diagnosis in certain patients. Poliomyelitis risk is only small except in parts of Yemen but rabies occurs throughout the region.

Those visiting Mecca and Medina should be aware that dehydration is common if the hajj coincides with the hot season and that many of the respiratory diseases (meningococcal meningitis, influenza) are more common where crowds meet together. Vaccination against meningo-coccal meningitis is essential when travelling to Saudi Arabia around the time of the hajj. Influenza vaccine may be a wise precaution.

Malaria is a low risk for most tourists to this region. In Oman, Syria and the UAE the risk is usually found only in rural regions. The sandfly-borne disease leishmaniasis occurs throughout the region but again the risk for tourists is small. Snake-bites and tick-borne diseases can occur in those who wander off the normal paths into the undergrowth in rural regions.

NORTHERN EUROPE

Common destinations: Belarus, Belgium, Czech Republic, Denmark, Finland, Germany, Ireland, Latvia, Luxembourg, Netherlands, Norway, Russia, Sweden and United Kingdom

Typical tourist vaccines (Eastern Europe): typhoid, poliomyelitis, tetanus and hepatitis A

For many reading *Travel in Health* this will be home and so the thought that health risks could occur while travelling in Europe will be surprising. However, when you leave your own area, travel risks do occur. Traffic accidents are commonly reported in travellers, so take special care when crossing roads and of course while driving.

Remember this region stretches from the west of Ireland to eastern Russia! Throughout this region many variations in climate occur and even this changes considerably throughout the year. Freezing winters coupled with scorching summers provide a fantastic variety of health problems for the unwary. Tapeworm infections (undercooked infected beef, pork and fish) are reported from some of the region and salmonella and other food-borne diseases can occur typically during the hotter summer months.

Even though malaria is not a problem (although transmission can occur) there are many other insect-borne diseases to be found. These include diseases associated with tick-bites like Lyme disease (widespread), tick-borne encephalitis (central Europe and as far north as Scandinavia) and tick-borne typhus (east and central Siberia). Contact with rodent urine (contamination of foods or through cuts) also may be associated with diseases like hantavirus or leptospirosis.

Poliomyelitis is very rare though diphtheria has been a problem in Russia, Belarus and Ukraine. Cases (mainly imported) have also been reported in Estonia, Finland, Latvia, Lithuania, Poland and Moldavia. Rabies in wild animals (mainly foxes) is endemic in most of the region.

SOUTHERN EUROPE

Common destinations: Albania, Andorra, Austria, Bosnia and Herzegovina, Bulgaria, France, Gibraltar, Greece, Hungary, Italy, Malta, Monaco, Portugal, Romania, Spain and Switzerland

Typical tourist vaccines (eastern parts): typhoid, poliomyelitis, tetanus and hepatitis A

Each year many hundreds of thousands of tourists descend upon this part of Europe. The standards of hygiene and available health care vary considerably throughout the region and again will vary with climatic conditions.

Bacillary dysentery and typhoid occur sporadically and are more common during the summer and autumn months. Brucellosis is found in the south-west and south-east of the region with hepatitis A in most countries. Salmonella and other food-borne diseases are increasing significantly in some of the countries.

Insect-borne diseases such as leishmaniasis (sandfly-borne), West Nile fever (mosquito-borne), typhus and Lyme disease (tick-borne) are all found to a variable degree in some of the countries.

Poliomyelitis transmission is rare but outbreaks have occurred in Albania (1996) which affected Greece and Yugoslavia. Hepatitis B is endemic (Albania, Bulgaria, Romania) and rabies occurs in most of the countries of southern Europe.

AUSTRALASIA

Common destinations: Australia and New Zealand

Typical tourist vaccines: None (except for those stopping off in transit in other risk regions)

Many tourists visiting these countries will stop off in some of the South-East Asian countries on their journey. Under these circumstances they will need to be aware of the potential risks involved even if only a short stay is involved.

In southern Australia the climate is somewhat similar to that of southern Europe and the same potential health risks are involved. However, jetlag is often a significant problem and sufficient rest must be taken to allow the body to adjust. Throughout the country the risk of food- and water-borne disease is small but during the hotter summer months food hygiene may be questionable when you are purchasing from street vendors. Dehydration and significant sun exposure can easily occur in the northern parts of the country during these times also.

Northern Australia has a wide variety of insect-borne diseases including Ross river fever and dengue fever (mosquito-borne) and typhus (tick-borne). Occasional outbreaks of Japanese B encephalitis (mosquito-borne) may occur in the northern part of the country around the Torres Strait.

Corals and jellyfish may present problems for the sea-bather, apart from the very occasional shark attacks which are reported. Some fruit- and insect-eating bats in Australia have been found to be infected with a virus similar to the rabies virus and so should be avoided.

New Zealand's islands provide a wide variety of climatic conditions throughout the year. Generally the risks are similar to those found in northern and southern European countries depending on the time of the year and the location throughout the country.

MELANESIA AND MICRONESIA–POLYNESIA

Common destinations: Samoa, Cook Islands, Fiji, Polynesia, Guam, Kiribati, Micronesia, New Caledonia, Papua New Guinea, Solomon Islands, Tonga and Vanuatu

Typical tourist vaccines: typhoid, poliomyelitis, tetanus and hepatitis A

This area covers a huge expanse of ocean and the countries included within this region vary considerably from smaller volcanic peaks to larger mountainous tropical rainforest-covered expanses.

Diarrhoeal diseases and typhoid occur and many of the worm conditions are also frequently reported. Poisoning from raw or undercooked fish and shellfish is also common and hepatitis A (food- and water-borne) and hepatitis B (sexually and blood-borne) are endemic.

Malaria occurs in Papua New Guinea, Solomon Islands and Vanuatu. Filariasis (mosquito-borne) is common throughout the region but varies greatly as a risk for tourists. Dengue fever (mosquito-borne) is found in most of the countries and epidemics frequently occur.

Poliomyelitis is very rare but hazards to sea-bathers still occur from poisonous fish and sea snakes. Dehydration and sun exposure can easily occur for the unwary.

INDEX

Acetazolamide, 96
acupuncture
  risks of, 29, 103
Addison's disease, 23
Afghanistan
  vaccines, 135
Africa
  infections, 76
  insect-borne diseases, 62
  rabies, 88
  trekking, 98
  vaccines, 26, 27, 28
    Northern, 123
    sub-Saharan, 124–5
AIDS, 27, 29, 103
  and vaccines, 23, 104
air conditioning
    insect protection, 65
Albania
  vaccines, 138
allergies, 36
  insect repellents, 40
altitude sickness, 130
  areas of risk, 94
  and asthma, 36
  and heart disease, 37
  planning for, 93–4
  risk factors, 93–7
  symptoms and signs, 94–6
  what to do, 96–7
altitudes, list of, 97
Amazon region
  vaccines, 130
amoeba, 114
amoebiasis, 128

amoebic dysentery
  eastern South Asia, 134
  middle South Asia, 135
Andes, 95
Andorra, 138
angina
  and altitude, 94
animals
  disease transmission, 76
  rabies transmission, 84–6
  as snake detectors, 91
antibiotics, 107
Antigua and Barbuda
  vaccines, 129
ants, 63–4
Arctic regions, 81
Argentina
  vaccines, 132
Armenia
  vaccines, 135
aromatherapy, 47
artemether, 70
Asia
  infections, 76
  vaccines, 25, 26, 27
    East, 133
    eastern South Asia, 134
    middle South Asia, 135
    western South Asia, 136
asthma, 36
  and altitude, 93, 94
  and vaccines, 23
athlete's foot, 115
Australasia
  vaccines, 139

Australia, 84, 139
Austria, 138
Azerbaijan
   vaccines, 135

bacillary dysentery
   Central America, 128
   eastern South Asia, 134
   middle South Asia, 135
   southern Europe, 138
Bahamas
   vaccines, 129
Bahrain
   vaccines, 136
Bangladesh
   vaccines, 135
Barbados
   vaccines, 129
bats
   rabies, 85, 139
bedbugs, 63
Belarus
   vaccines, 137
Belgium, 137
Belize
   vaccines, 128
Bermuda, 127
bilharzia. see schistosomiasis
blood transfusion, 103
boats, 76, 100
body-piercing, 103
Bolivia
   vaccines, 130–131
Bombay, 86
Bosnia and Herzegovina
   vaccines, 138
Botswana
   vaccines, 126
bottled drinks, 57–8
bowel parasitic disease, 116, 132, 133

bowel problems, 114
Brazil
   vaccines, 130–131
breastfeeding
   and vaccines, 23
brucellosis, 53, 117
   East Asia, 133
   middle South Asia, 135
   southern Europe, 138
   western South Asia, 136
Brunei
   vaccines, 134
Bulgaria
   vaccines, 138
bus travel, 100–101

Cambodia
   vaccines, 134
Canada, 127
cancellations, 41
Cape Town, SA, 126
Caribbean region
   vaccines, 129
Cayman Islands
   vaccines, 129
CDC, 72
Central Africa
   vaccines, 124–5
Central America
   rabies, 85, 88
   trekking, 98
   vaccines, 27, 128
checklist, 38–42
   medical, 5, 41
children
   dehydration, 105
   fevers, 106
   rabies protection, 85
   scorpion sting, 92
   travelling with, 33–4

Chile
  vaccines, 132
China
  vaccines, 133
chloroquine, 70
cholera, 18–19, 51
  eastern South Asia, 134
  middle South Asia, 135
  temperate South America, 132
  vaccine, 25
chopsticks, 52
chronic fatigue syndrome, 116–17
circadian rhythm, 47
clothing
  infection of, 99–100, 115
  trekking, 99–100
cockroaches, 63–4
cold food, 50
Colombia
  vaccines, 130–131
condoms, 103
conjunctivitis
  swimming pools, 75
consulates, 110
contact names, 41
Cook Islands
  vaccines, 140
corals, 139
crocodiles, 77, 100
cryptosporidia, 114
Cuba
  vaccines, 129
currency, 40, 120
cutlery, 52
Cyprus
  vaccines, 136
cystitis, 116
Czech Republic
  vaccines, 137

dairy produce, 53
Darussalam
  vaccines, 134
DEET, 64
dehydration, 109, 126, 136
  diarrhoea, 105
  fevers, 107
dengue fever, 61
  Australia, 139
  Caribbean, 129
  Central America, 128
  Melanesia/Micronesia, 140
  middle South Asia, 135
Denmark, 137
dentistry, 103
destination, choice of, 3–5
diabetes, 34–5
  and altitude, 94
  and vaccines, 23
diarrhoea, 48, 140
  medical attention, 109
  post-travel, 114
  treatment, 105–6, 107
diet
  and jetlag, 47
diethyl toluamide (DEET), 64
diphtheria
  northern Europe, 137
  sub-Saharan Africa, 125
  vaccine, 27
disease
  food-borne, 48–54
  human contacts, 101, 102–4, 117, 136
  insect-borne, 60–66
  sexually transmitted, 102–4, 117
  water-borne, 55–9
Dominican Republic
  vaccines, 129
doxycycline, 71

driving, 126, 127, 137
drug allergies
    and vaccines, 23
dysentery, 109
    eastern South Asia, 134
    middle South Asia, 135
    southern Europe, 138

ear-piercing, 103
earplugs, 78
East Asia
    vaccines, 133
Eastern Europe
    vaccines, 137
Ecuador, 37, 94
    vaccines, 130–131
eczema
    and vaccines, 23
egg allergy
    and vaccines, 24
Egypt
    vaccines, 123
El Salvador
    vaccines, 128
electricity, 6–8
embassies, 110
encephalitis, 61
    Australia, 139
    middle South Asia, 135
    northern Europe, 137
    vaccine, 28
epilepsy
    and vaccines, 23
essential oils, 47
Estonia
    vaccines, 137
Europe
    northern, 137
    southern, 138
exercise
    and jetlag, 46

Far East
    food contamination, 51
    vaccines, 25, 133
fever
    medical attention, 110
    treatment of, 106–7
Fiji
    vaccines, 140
filariasis, 61
    Melanesia/Micronesia, 140
    middle South Asia, 135
Finland, 137
first aid, 105–8
first-aid kit, 4, 110
    list, 20–21
fish, raw, 51
fleas, 63
flies, 52
fluid intake, 34
    and jetlag, 46
    necessity of, 55–6
    and sunburn, 83, 106
food allergies
    and vaccines, 24
food-borne disease, 48–54
France, 138
freshwater swimming, 76–7, 116
fruit, 52, 101
fruit drinks, 58
fungal infections, 115

Galapagos Islands, 130
Gambia
    vaccines, 124–5
gastroenteritis, 132
Germany, 137
Ghana
    vaccines, 124–5
giardia, 114
Gibraltar, 138

glasses, prescription for, 40
golf courses
   mosquito risk, 61
gonorrhoea, 103, 117
Greece, 81, 138
Grenada
   vaccines, 129
Guam
   vaccines, 140
Guatemala
   vaccines, 128
guidebooks, 40

halofantrine, 70
hantavirus, 137
headache, 109
heart disease, 37
   and altitude, 93, 94
hepatitis, 29
hepatitis A, 51
   Caribbean, 129
   Central America, 128
   East Asia, 133
   Eastern Europe, 137
   eastern South Asia, 134
   Melanesia/Micronesia, 140
   middle South Asia, 135
   Northern Africa, 123
   Southern Africa, 126
   southern Europe, 138
   sub-Saharan Africa, 124-5
   temperate South America, 132
   tropical South America, 130-131
   vaccine, 27-8
   western South Asia, 136
hepatitis B, 103
   East Asia, 133
   Melanesia/Micronesia, 140
   southern Europe, 138
   sub-Saharan Africa, 125

vaccine, 27
hepatitis E
   eastern South Asia, 134
   middle South Asia, 135
herpes virus, 103, 117
Himalayas, 95
hippos, 77
HIV, 117
holiday representatives, 110
'holiday tablets,' 41
homeopathy, 29-30
Honduras
   vaccines, 128
Hong Kong
   vaccines, 133
hookworm, 115
hot food, 49-50
Hungary, 138
hydrophobia, 85
hyper-tension
   and altitude, 94
hypoglycaemia, 35

ice, 57, 58
ice cream, 53
India
   mosquitoes, 68
   rabies, 88
   trekking, 98
   vaccines, 24-5, 26, 135
Indonesia
   vaccines, 134
influenza, 136
injections, 107
insect bites, 29
insect repellents, 40, 64-5
insect-borne diseases, 60-66
   protection against bites, 64-5
   what to do if bitten, 65
insurance, travel, 38

Internet cafes, 110
Iran
    vaccines, 135
Ireland, 84, 137
Israel
    vaccines, 136
Italy, 138
itinerary, copy of, 42

Jamaica
    vaccines, 129
Japan
    vaccines, 133
Japanese B encephalitis, 61
    Australia, 139
    middle South Asia, 135
    vaccine, 28
jellyfish, 129, 139
jetlag, 139
    rules for, 45–7
jogging
    rabies risk, 86–7
Johannesburg, SA, 126
Jordan
    vaccines, 136

Kenya
    vaccines, 124–5
Kiribati
    vaccines, 140
kitchens, checking, 48–9
Korea
    vaccines, 133
Kruger National Park, SA, 126
Kuwait
    vaccines, 136

lake swimming, 76–7, 116
Laos
    vaccines, 134

larva migrans, 115, 129
Latvia
    vaccines, 137
Lebanon
    vaccines, 136
leeches
    eastern South Asia, 134
    tropical South America, 130
leishmaniasis, 62, 116
    middle South Asia, 135
    southern Europe, 138
    western South Asia, 136
leptospirosis
    eastern South Asia, 134
    northern Europe, 137
Lesotho
    vaccines, 126
Lithuania
    vaccines, 137
lizards, 63–4
Luxembourg, 137
Lyme disease, 63, 116
    northern Europe, 137
    southern Europe, 138
    USA, 127

Machu Picchu, 130
malaria, 14–15, 33, 61, 107
    areas of risk
        Caribbean, 129
        Central America, 128
        eastern South Asia, 134
        Melanesia/Micronesia, 140
        middle South Asia, 135
        sub-Saharan Africa, 124–5
        temperate South America, 132
        western South Asia, 136
    diagnosis, 69
    killing disease, 72
    life cycle, 67

prophylaxis, 70–73
risk of, 67–73
signs and symptoms, 68–9, 114
standby treatment, 69–70
tablets, 28, 32, 39, 67–8, 70–73
    reasons to take, 71–3
    types of, 70–71
Malawi
    vaccines, 124–5
Malaysia
    vaccines, 134
Maldives
    vaccines, 135
Malta, 138
Mauritius
    vaccines, 124–5
Mecca, 136
medical attention, 109–10
medical check, 5, 118–19
Medina, 136
mefloquine, 70
Mekong delta, Vietnam, 134
Melanesia
    vaccines, 140
melanin, 81
melanomas, 82
melatonin, 47
meningitis, 109
    sub-Saharan Africa, 125
meningococcal meningitis, 28
    middle South Asia, 135
    western South Asia, 136
Mexico
    vaccines, 24–5, 128
Micronesia-Polynesia
    vaccines, 140
Middle East
    vaccines, 136
migraine
    and altitude, 94

mineral waters, 57, 101
minerals, 57–8
mobile phones, 41
Moldavia
    vaccines, 137
moles
    and sunburn, 82
Monaco, 138
Morocco
    vaccines, 123
mosquito net, 64, 65, 100
mosquitoes, 61. see also malaria
    dengue fever, 128, 129, 139, 140
    filariasis, 135
    West Nile fever, 138
motoring, 126, 127, 137
Mount Kenya, 95–6
Mozambique, 126

Namibia
    vaccines, 126
nausea, 41
    treatment, 107
neck stiffness, 107, 109
needles, infected, 103, 107
neighbours, informing, 41
Nepal
    altitude, 94
    rabies, 88
    trekking, 98
    vaccines, 28, 135
Netherlands, 137
New Caledonia
    vaccines, 140
New Zealand, 84, 139
Nicaragua
    vaccines, 128
Nigeria
    vaccines, 124–5
Nile river, 123

North America, 127
Northern Africa
    vaccines, 123
Norway, 137

Okavango region, Botswana, 126
Oman
    vaccines, 136

Pakistan
    vaccines, 135
Panama
    vaccines, 128
panic attacks
    and altitude, 93
Papua New Guinea
    vaccines, 140
paracetamol, 106
passports, 39, 120
Peru
    vaccines, 130–131
Philippines
    vaccines, 134
photographs, 120
planning ahead, 120
Poland
    vaccines, 137
poliomyelitis, 51
    Caribbean, 129
    East Asia, 133
    Eastern Europe, 137
    eastern South Asia, 134
    Melanesia/Micronesia, 140
    middle South Asia, 135
    Northern Africa, 123
    Southern Africa, 126
    southern Europe, 138
    sub-Saharan Africa, 124–5
    vaccine, 25–6
    western South Asia, 136

Polynesia
    vaccines, 140
Portugal, 81, 138
post-travel
    medical care, 113–17
    medical check, 118–19
    next trip, 120
pregnancy, 31–3
    and altitude, 94
    and vaccines, 23
proguanil, 70
protozoa, 50
psoriasis
    and vaccines, 23
pyrimethamine-sulphonamide, 70

quinine, 70
Quito, Ecuador, 37, 130

rabies, 34, 84–9
    areas of risk, 84
        high risk, 86–7
    transmission of, 84–6
    urgency of treatment, 88
    vaccine, 26, 87, 88, 133
        Australia, 139
        Caribbean, 129
        Central America, 128
        East Asia, 133
        Eastern South Asia, 134
        middle South Asia, 135
        Northern Africa, 123
        northern Europe, 137
        southern Europe, 138
        sub-Saharan Africa, 125
        tropical South America, 130
        USA, 127
        western South Asia, 136
    what to do if bitten, 87
rainfall, 11–12

relapsing fever, 116
Rift Valley, 95
river swimming, 76–7, 116
robbery, 101, 127
Romania
    vaccines, 138
Ross river fever
    Australia, 139
Russia
    vaccines, 137

St Louis encephalitis, 61
salmonella, 138
salt depletion, 55–6, 106
Samoa
    vaccines, 140
sandflies, 61–2, 116
    middle South Asia, 135
    Northern Africa, 123
    southern Europe, 138
    tropical South America, 130
    western South Asia, 136
sarcoidosis
    and vaccines, 23
Saudi Arabia
    vaccines, 136
scabies, 115–16
Scandinavia, 84
schistosomiasis, 76–7, 100, 114, 116
    East Asia, 133
    eastern South Asia, 134
    middle South Asia, 135
    Northern Africa, 123
    sub-Saharan Africa, 124–5
scorpions, 92, 126
scuba-diving, 5
    and asthma, 36
    risks, 76
sea bathing, 75–6, 139, 140
sea snakes, 91, 140

sea urchins, 129
security, 101, 126, 127, 131
sex tourism, 103
sexually transmitted disease, 102–4,
    117
Seychelles
    vaccines, 124–5
sharks, 139
shellfish, 51
Siberia
    vaccines, 137
Singapore
    vaccines, 134
skin cancer, 82
skin problems, 107, 110, 115
smuggling
    animals, 89
snakes, 90–91
    Central America, 128
    eastern South Asia, 134
    middle South Asia, 135
    Southern Africa, 126
    western South Asia, 136
Solomon Islands
    vaccines, 140
South Africa
    vaccines, 126
South America, 76
    rabies, 85, 88
    vaccines, 25, 27
        temperate, 132
        tropical, 130–131
Southern Africa
    vaccines, 126
Spain, 81, 138
spiders, 91
Sri Lanka
    vaccines, 135
St Kitts and Nevis
    vaccines, 129

St Lucia
  vaccines, 129
steroids
  and vaccines, 104
stir-fry meals, 51
stomach upsets, 41
street vendors, 126, 130
  food, 53–4
Sub-Saharan Africa
  vaccines, 124–5
Sulawesi, Indonesia, 134
sunburn, 33, 79–83
  areas of risk, 81
    Australasia, 139
    Caribbean, 129
    Melanesia/Micronesia, 140
    Northern Africa, 123
    tropical South America, 130
  protection advice, 83
  reasons for, 81
  skin cancer, 82
  skin types, 80
  sun block, 40, 83
  times of day, 80–81
  treatment, 106
  warning signs, 82
Swaziland
  vaccines, 126
Sweden, 137
swimmer's itch, 116
swimming, 74–8, 100, 129
swimming pools, 74–5
Switzerland, 138
symptoms, 113–17
syphilis, 103
Syria
  vaccines, 136

taeniasis, 136
Tajikistan
  vaccines, 135

Tanzania
  vaccines, 124–5
tap water, 56
tapeworm infestation, 50
  northern Europe, 137
  temperate South America, 132
  western South Asia, 136
teeth, brushing
  contamination risk, 58–9
telephone cards, 40
temperatures, 9–10
tetanus, 26
  Caribbean, 129
  Central America, 128
  East Asia, 133
  Eastern Europe, 137
  eastern South Asia, 134
  Melanesia/Micronesia, 140
  middle South Asia, 135
  Northern Africa, 123
  Southern Africa, 126
  southern Europe, 138
  sub-Saharan Africa, 124–5
  temperate South America, 132
  tropical South America, 130–131
  western South Asia, 136
tetracycline, 71
Thailand
  trekking, 98
  vaccines, 24–5, 134
thieves, 101, 127
tickbite fever, 63
ticks, 62–3, 116
  Australia, 139
  middle South Asia, 135
  northern Europe, 137
  Southern Africa, 126
  USA, 127
  western South Asia, 136
time zones, 13
  and diabetes, 35

jetlag, 45, 46
tissue myiasis, 115
Tonga
    vaccines, 140
torch, 65, 99
train travel, 100–101
travel agents, 38
travel insurance, 38
trekking, 98–101
    bites and stings, 99
    clothing, 99–100
    food and water, 99
    rabies, 86–7, 88
    ticks, 62–3
Trinidad and Tobago
    vaccines, 129
trypanosomiasis, 62
tsetse flies, 62
tuberculosis, 53, 117
Tunisia
    vaccines, 123
Turkey
    vaccines, 136
typhoid, 51, 53
    Caribbean, 129
    Central America, 128
    East Asia, 133
    Eastern Europe, 137
    eastern South Asia, 134
    Melanesia/Micronesia, 140
    middle South Asia, 135
    Northern Africa, 123
    Southern Africa, 126
    southern Europe, 138
    sub-Saharan Africa, 124–5
    temperate South America, 132
    tropical South America, 130–131
    vaccine, 26
    western South Asia, 136

typhus, 63, 116
    Australia, 139
    northern Europe, 137
    southern Europe, 138

Ukraine
    vaccines, 137
United Arab Emirates, 136
United Kingdom, 84, 137
United States of America (USA), 127
    insect-borne diseases, 63
    rabies, 84
urinary tract problems, 116
Uruguay
    vaccines, 132

vaccination, need for, 39
vaccination card, 120
vaccines, 22–30
    alternatives to, 28–30
    contraindications, 23–4, 104
    descriptions of, 25–8
    essential/recommended, 24–5
    and pregnancy, 32
    rabies, 87, 88
    requirements, 4
    side effects, 24
Vanuatu
    vaccines, 140
Venezuela
    vaccines, 130–131
Victoria Falls, 124
Vietnam
    vaccines, 134
Virgin Islands
    vaccines, 129
visas, 4, 38–9
voltages, 6–7

vomiting
    medical attention, 109
    treatment, 107

water fountains, 58
water jug, 56–7
water-borne disease, 55–9
Weil's disease, 134
West Africa
    vaccines, 25
West Nile fever, 138
World Health Organisation (WHO),
        25, 48, 72

yellow fever, 61
    Central America, 128
    countries affected, 16–17

sub-Saharan Africa, 124–5
tropical South America, 130–131
vaccine, 25
Yemen
    vaccines, 136
Yugoslavia, 138

Zambia
    vaccines, 124–5
Zimbabwe
    mosquitoes, 68
    vaccines, 124–5